CHRISTIAN
MANIFESTO

CHRISTIAN MANIFESTO

Ernest T. Campbell

HARPER & ROW, PUBLISHERS
New York, Evanston, and London

1817

FIRST EDITION

LIBRARY OF CONGRESS CATALOG CARD NUMBER: 78-109069

TO MY FATHER AND MOTHER,
IRELAND'S GIFT TO AMERICA
AND GOD'S GIFT TO ME

CONTENTS

PREFACE

Some Christians believe that the gospel has *nothing* to do with the world. Others that the gospel has *only* to do with the world. Still others that the gospel must be related *both* to the world *and* to men and women in it. In earlier years I entered uncritically into the first of these positions. In recent years I have been tempted to cast my lot with the second. The conviction is strong within me and growing, however, that the third position is the only one that does justice to our faith and keeps us on speaking terms with common sense.

I would not presume to commit this conviction to print did I not believe that the Christian church in these United States is confronted by no more menacing danger than the danger of coming apart on the question of whether the gospel is personal or social. Our ranks, all too thin to begin with, are being sorely and needlessly divided on this issue. One side tends to suspect the Christian credentials of the other. The cause is being hobbled by an intramural dispute.

Most of the books turned out in recent years by those who would see the church an active agent for political and social change have, in the main, been insensitive to what Jesus Christ means to men and women who know Him as a vital, saving, living presence. The vertical dimension of Christianity has been all but ignored in the rush to implement the horizontal dimension. In short, one author after another has leapfrogged over a sizable company of convincible and potentially influential Christians by opening the conversation at a point too far down the line from where his brethren live.

Labels are precarious appendages to reality and frequently serve as a substitute for thought. Since God is the only public that ultimately matters, I have long since given up worrying about how others choose to classify my life and work. It belongs to my hopes for this book, however, to identify myself as one who takes the Bible seriously and believes without reservation in the power of the Christian gospel to change human nature.

At the same time, I contend that evangelicals in this country have limited the gospel, impeded its proclamation, and hindered its acceptance by refusing to be concerned with political and social justice. If a few who share my respect for the evangelical tradition can be moved through these pages to faith in a larger Christ and a more significant involvement in history, this volume will not have been in vain.

CHRISTIAN
      MANIFESTO

CHAPTER I

The Option We Tend to Forget

The Moderator of the Presbytery comes down gently with his gavel and politely announces that the floor debate going on will have to be arrested because time has come on the docket for the judicatory to listen to an address on the inner city by a guest minister. The announcement touches off a stir in the assembly, and before the speaker can be introduced by the chairman of the Church in Society Committee a sizable number of commissioners push for the doors and a chance to catch a breath of air outside.

Two months later the Presbytery meets again. Prime time on *this* docket has been allocated to the Committee on Evangelism. At the appointed hour the chairman representing this concern gets up to announce that his report will center in a filmstrip designed to help train laymen in the art of sharing their faith with others. As the house lights darken, a significant number of commissioners—not the ones who bolted the previous meeting—slip up the aisles and out of sight.

Examples in the extreme? Perhaps. But something like this

has been happening with alarming frequency over the past ten years in presbyteries, associations, conferences, and dioceses across the country. Rival camps have been shaping up and viewing each other with unsettling misgivings. The pietists who hold that the only business of the church is to win men to Christ and nurture them in the faith see their action-oriented colleagues as part of a conspiracy that threatens to scuttle the faith and reduce the church to just another pressure group. Those who wish to see the social and political implications of the gospel woven into the warp and woof of American life see the evangelistic enterprise as a grossly irrelevant holdover from a day that has long since passed. Positions quickly harden and communication breaks down. New men are typed on arrival. A dialectic sets in where genuine dialogue should be taking place.

Laymen, too, share in the tension and confusion. During a political hassle on a fair housing ordinance in one of our major cities, this irate letter found its way to the editorial page of the local newspaper: "The best thing the City Council can do is to drop the entire matter. Regarding the Council of Churches, the church and state are separate. Therefore the church should mind its own business. The business of the church is to preach the gospel of Jesus Christ and save the souls of sinners. If the church will do this it will not have time to meddle in anything else." The letter was signed, not insignificantly, "Owner of Income Property."

Lots of laymen resent the introduction of contemporary social problems into public worship. A church in Brooklyn that works hard to unite the "in here" with the "out there" when it gathers for worship, includes in its order of service a reading from the Old Testament, a reading from the New Testament, and a reading from the "Now Testament." This last might be a paragraph from the Kerner Report, or word about some program recently launched for the benefit of the community. A growing number of churches include a "Moment of Concern" in their services of worship. The concern might be a report on some bill pending in the state legislature, an invitation for members to participate in a voter registration drive, or something of the kind.

Most common of all, however, are prayers, litanies, and sermons that increasingly bring the realities of human need into the act of worship itself. Such developments are resented and resisted by worshipers who have come to look upon the sanctuary as a place where one might find release from the moil and turmoil of the world. When the very place of refuge proves to be both disturbed and disturbing, what is one to do? Many in the main-line churches have sought to worship elsewhere, perhaps in a church of Fundamentalist leanings where current issues are seldom broached. The problem here is that churches in this tradition, more often than not, will not satisfy the disgruntled churchman's taste for good music, intellectually stimulating preaching, and a well-ordered service of worship. Tragically he becomes a man without a church home—and his name is legion.

Members who are wrought up over the church's forays into matters deemed by them to be beyond its mandate often move to make their feelings known by cutting back their gifts. They vote, as it were, by pledge card. It is true, generally speaking, that over the past decades more daring and imaginative programs in such fields as race relations and poverty have been launched by denominations at the national level than by local churches at the parish level. This is so not only because national bodies have the ability to engage specialists, but because resistance to novelty and experimentation is more acute at the corner of Main and Spruce than it is at 475 Riverside Drive.

Denominational boards and agencies are fast becoming prime targets of those who choose to speak through withheld funds. Ostensibly, benevolence funds for the church's general mission are cut in order to make a burgeoning bureaucracy thin ranks. Actually, one fears, the real reason is to curtail innovative and provocative programs and bring the leaders of the church to heel.

It is common for pulpit nominating committees to inquire diligently into the evangelistic inclinations and social leanings of potential candidates for vacant churches. Church magazines that run articles dealing with the inner life, or summoning Christians to be more zealous in their personal witnessing for Christ, will draw a fiery mail response from those who view such pieces as evasions of reality. Similarly, printed appeals for heartier participation in political and social issues will raise the dander of readers who question the right of the church to become embroiled in controversial subjects. Eventually, pastors and congregations of like mind find each other, with the result that in one town after another from Maine to California, local churches are tabbed as "spiritual" or "worldly," "out of it" or "with it." These designations have a way of becoming more significant, to laymen and ministers alike, than formal denominational pedigrees.

An equally ominous division has been eating into the unity of the Roman Catholic Church. So much is this the case that responsible analysts of the religious scene in America suggest that new coalitions may presently be formalized in the Christian community which will see liberal Protestant and Roman Catholic Christians joining to offset a union of conservatively oriented Christians of both traditions. And this at a time when a divided world fairly cries for a united church! Uniformity we do not want, but without fundamental unity how can we address ourselves to the Father's business?

Elmer Wheeler tells of a druggist who was dissatisfied with the profit he was making on his soda fountain. What to do? He decided to push the idea that a good malted ought to be enriched with an egg. To plant the suggestion, he instructed his clerks to ask their malted milk customers, "Would you like an egg in your malted?" Nothing much happened. Receipts stayed where they were. Presently he got the bright idea to change the question. Under new instructions the clerks were to face their malted customers with an egg in each hand and ask, "Would you like one egg or two?" Receipts began to rise. Under pressure of the question as revised, buyers tended to lose sight of their other option—no egg at all!

The church, in the matter under discussion here, is suffering the pains of a forgotten option. There is no reason, theological or otherwise, why a minister, a layman, or a congregation should have to choose between the equally valid claims of those who want to see Christ enthroned in the hearts of men and those who are determined to Christify the world. Neither side can bear a full-orbed witness to the gospel without the other. To tune a television set properly one must adjust both the *Vertical Hold* and *Horizontal Hold* buttons. For the church to beam a full and representative picture of Christ to the world she must be vertically alive to God and horizontally in touch with men and all that troubles them.

One senses a mounting willingness to acknowledge that Protestantism in this country has spent more time fingering the *Vertical Hold* control than the *Horizontal*. Fundamentalism, for example, has seldom addressed itself to issues that partake of economic or political reality. It has sought to operate in a spiritual vacuum, as though history were not really there. Fundamentalists generally either retreat from history by concentrating on the inner life or make the equally damaging mistake of uncritically defending a given political or economic order on the assumption that it is God-ordained. Those who maximize the "world within" will be found singing the "old" hymns of the church that speak of inner peace and hint at the wonders of the world to come. The others are likely to be found among the superpatriots who brand every attempt to modify the system as Communist-inspired. They give the impression of being Americans who happen to be Christians, rather than Christians who happen to be Americans.

By any reckoning, it is indeed a sticky question to what degree and in what form the Christian church should participate in the give-and-take of history. What is heartening is that a new willingness to pursue this question is emerging. The Congress on Evangelism held in Minneapolis in September of 1969 was marked by a gratifying determination on the part of evangelicals to search out the social implications of the Christian message.

Experience teaches me that both "sides" need each other. I remember an afternoon conference in my study in which four or five rather well-known ministers who had established a reputation for sustained and courageous action in the civil rights struggle met to reflect on steps to be taken next. At the coffee break we fell to reminiscing about our beginnings in the Christian faith. Each man in that room, without exception, owed his start in the Christian life to some church or pastor of evangelical persuasion who cared enough about Jesus Christ to share Him with others. A central loyalty was cast that had served as a sheet anchor in the time of storm and a durable foundation on which to build an ever-broadening Christian life. One owes an abiding debt to the tradition in which his eyes were made to see. Shakespeare's words will surely find the man who grows too big for his beginnings.

> Lowliness is young ambition's ladder,
> Whereto the climber-upward turns his face;
> But when he once attains the upmost round,
> He then unto the ladder turns his back,
> Looks in the clouds, scorning the base degrees
> By which he did ascend . . .[1]

A church so busily at work correcting the massive injustices of society that it cannot or will not make the effort to win men and women to an allegiance to Jesus Christ will soon become sterile and unable to produce after its kind. My years in the church have impressed on me the fact that candidates for the ministry and other forms of Christian service come in greatest numbers from local churches that believe in confronting their young people with the claims of Jesus Christ. People who could not muster an ounce of devotion for such abstractions as justice, peace, or freedom will often commit their very lives to Jesus Christ, once the overwhelming implications of His death for them upon a cross begin to grip their hearts. Within the context of this loyalty the cause of justice, peace, and freedom takes on a new compulsion.

The other side of the coin is that churches in the conservative theological tradition are in danger of losing their sons and daughters by their failure to reckon seriously with history. Throughout my ministry I have known the exhilaration that comes with serving near a college or university. I have counseled by the hour with young people in their late teens or early twenties who were so disillusioned with what their church back home did not tell them or prepare them for that they were ready to chuck the whole business. One can only surmise that for every one who sought out counseling there were dozens who just gave up and stole away without consulting anyone. This phenomenon, which hundreds of pastors could attest, was what prompted us to say as part of our response to "The Christian Manifesto"[2] that a counterclaim "for compensation might be made by many churches in the land for time spent attempting to counsel the casualties of fundamentalism back to spiritual health."

It is not enough to liken the Christian enterprise to a ride on a railroad train with every passenger having only the duty of getting others to come on board. Somewhere along the line the overall purpose of the trip must be searched and the relationship between train and surrounding countryside studied. Attention must be given to the question of why some on board enjoy first-class comfort in the privacy of a roomette while others swelter in an overcrowded coach.

The church is not an end in itself. It is meant to be an instrument of God for the work that He wants done here and now. To liken it to a railroad train (or ark) and suggest that the sole responsibility of those inside is to invite others in is to opt for a church that sees salvation as an end in itself and not the means it was meant to be. When young people are made to feel that they must leave the church if they wish to plunge into the major problems that beset the human race, then clearly the theology of that church stands condemned.

One is encouraged in his travels around the church by the growing number of local parishes and ministers who want to be persuaded, on theological grounds, that a witness to the gospel must be borne in secular affairs. The truth is slowly but surely coming home that the church by its very existence is already and unavoidably in politics. Failure to act translates out as an endorsement of the way things are. This was the point of Professor Mogey's criticism of the Ulster government when he wrote: "I want to argue that the Government of Northern Ireland may be said to have failed, not because of anything it has done over the years, but because of what it has never recognized it had to do."[3]

The earnest contention now threatening to fragment the church beyond recognition could very well be prelude to a new unity in which the people of God pursue with equal dedication the joys of heaven and the cares of earth. Walter Rauschenbusch many years ago unfurled a banner beneath which all might march together, when he wrote: "There are two great entities in human life, the human soul and the human race,—and religion is to save both. The soul is to seek righteousness and eternal life, and the race is to seek righteousness and the Kingdom of God."[4]

CHAPTER II

Lord of What?

In a world where the whirring maw of the computer conspires to dehumanize us all, and numbers—more than names—carry the frail cargo of our personal identity into the bulging files of government and business, it is reassuring to touch down in the Gospels and find that Jesus of Nazareth had time for people on a personal basis. We seem never to tire of listening in on Jesus' conversations—with the woman at the well, with Nicodemus, with Zacchaeus, with Mary and Martha, with the rich young ruler, with Peter, and a host of others. Apparently he took the time we claim we do not have.

It would be fair to say that before religious experience is anything else it is personal interaction between the soul and God. A man must live to God firsthand. The Christian claim is that Christ still encounters men. The Great Physician, as Kierkegaard enjoyed recounting,[1] moves among earth's sick, imploring, "Come unto me, all ye that labour and are heavy laden, and I will give you rest" (Matt. 11:28, AV).*

The overture being personally delivered and addressed, the

*Scripture quotations, unless otherwise indicated, are from the Revised Standard Version.

response must be personal too. It belongs to the evangelistic aspect of the church's mission to entreat men to "receive Jesus Christ as their personal Savior." It is by an individual act of faith, produced through nurture or conversion, that the grace of God is appropriated unto salvation.

It would be hard to imagine a closer relationship between two persons than the relationship the New Testament insists can prevail between the soul and Jesus Christ. One is not a Christian because he subscribes to "it"—that is, to Christianity as a system of thought or a set of principles. One is not a Christian because he believes in "her"—that is, the church as a venerable and laudatory institution in society. One is a Christian because he believes in "Him," the God-man Jesus Christ, and is conscious of His presence in the heart.

New Testament religion is not private, but it is personal. This point is worth contending for in a day when distinguished churchmen of virtually every tradition seem committed to the view that the Christian faith needs only to be realigned institutionally to become once more a first-rate power in the world. No reshuffling of lifeless adherents to Christianity is likely to produce results worthy of an arched eyebrow or a second look.

James S. Stewart would have us eternally in his debt had his only offering to the world been the book *A Man in Christ*.[2] There he hammers home the indisputable fact that believers in the early church knew themselves and each other as men and women "in Christ." In one form or another this dynamic designation appears no less than 164 times in the New Testament. The term "Christian," on the other hand, appears only three times and in each instance is applied to those early believers by outsiders.

Would it be unfair to suggest that in passing from the term "in Christ" to "Christian" to "Christianity" to "Christendom" we have fallen further and further away from the power we were meant to have? Webster's unabridged dictionary lists four main definitions of the word "Christian."

1. A person who professes belief in Jesus as the Christ—or in the religion based on the teachings of Jesus.

2. The chief character in *Pilgrim's Progress*.

3. A decent, respectable person.

4. In a general sense, anyone born of Christian parents.

How easily we drop from number one to number four. And what a price we pay for doing so! Wilfred Cantwell Smith puts his finger squarely on the matter when he notes,

It is as Christians' faith in God has weakened that they have busied themselves with Christianity; and as their personal relation to Christ has virtually lapsed that they have turned to religion for solace. The notion that religion is a nice thing to have, even that it is useful, has arisen, as it could arise, only in a secular and desperate society. Such a notion is a kind of blasphemy to those whose faith is sensitive. One has even reached a point today where some Christians can speak of believing in Christianity (instead of believing in God and in Christ); of preaching Christianity (instead of preaching good news, salvation, redemption); of practising Christianity (instead of practising love). Some even talk of being saved by Christianity, instead of by the only thing that could possibly save us, the anguish and the love of God.[3]

The term "personal savior" as such is not to be found in Scripture. However, the concept behind it holds clear title to a prominent place in Christian thought. The claims of Christianity remain abstract and sterile until a man comes to see himself as the object of God's forgiving love. Healing is on the way when an individual becomes aware that *his* sin, not just sin in general, drove the nails into those sinless hands and impaled the son of God upon the cross.

When the gospel is *proclaimed* it sounds the heartening word that "God so loved the *world*" (John 3:16). When the gospel is *received* it becomes ecstatically personal: "He loved *me* and gave Himself for *me*" (Gal. 2:20).

But it is an equally and inseparably urgent assertion of the Christian faith that Jesus Christ is Lord as well as savior. Both terms are crucial to a genuine experience of Christ. *Passively* a man accepts Jesus as his savior. He did for us what we could never do for ourselves. *Actively,* he rises up to follow Him as Lord. Thus, a Christian oscillates between an awareness of what Christ has done for him and what he may do for Christ. When the saviorhood of Jesus is stressed to the neglect of his Lordship as the Christ and all that this implies, the gospel is distorted, and Christian living becomes an indulgence in privilege easily divorced from responsible ethical behavior. We are summoned to obey as Lord the one whom we gratefully receive as savior. We are not only *objects* of salvation, but *instruments* of salvation as well. We must "go" as well as "come."

The earliest Christian creed of all is the terse affirmation, "Jesus Christ is Lord." This is the kerygma about which so much has been written in recent years, the core message of the church. It is the cardinal claim of the New Testament. But "Lord of What?" we might ask. Lord of my life, to be sure. A servant is one who is at the disposal of his master, and a Christian one who places himself at the disposal of Jesus Christ. We yield up our sovereignty to a will that is higher than our own. As St. Paul put it, "He died for all, that those who live might live no longer for themselves but for him who for their sake died and was raised" (II Cor. 5:15). Life for the Christian is a "command performance." Christ becomes the organizing center of his being and the star by which he sees.

But more than this, when we hail Jesus Christ as Lord, we acknowledge Him to be Lord of the church as well. Clearly this is what the Apostle is affirming when he writes, "Rather, speaking the truth in love, we are to grow up in every way into him who is the head, into Christ" (Eph. 4:15). Christ is to His church what the head is to the body. In Roman Catholic theology the Pope stands only as "vicar" or representative of the one whose authority is all-prevailing, Jesus Christ. The implications of this truth are timely and far-reaching, but to track them now would be to wander off the fairway and lose sight of the green.

Lord of my life. Lord of the church. And Lord of history, too. We dare not so interpret the Lordship of Christ as to overlook His cosmic significance. He has a will for individual men and women *and for the world in which they live.*

The salvation that Jesus wrought by His life, death, and resurrection cannot be interpreted in exclusively personal terms if we wish to keep faith with the New Testament. The first Adam in his fall affected *all* of God's creation. The last Adam, Jesus Christ, set out to "reconcile all things to God in heaven and on earth" (Col. 1:20).

Christ as the Logos, a theme joyfully celebrated and elaborated in the prologue to St. John's Gospel, hints at the universal character of the Word that proceeds eternally from the mouth of God. To the Christ is attributed the creation of all things. His work is not limited in the old dispensation to the covenant community (Israel), for His truth is the light that illumines every man that comes into the world.

The finality of Christ is an inclusive and not an exclusive finality. It is not the case that what we find in Him is altogether discontinuous with religious insights that men in every place and time have garnered through the years. Rather, we find in Jesus Christ the unique focus and embodiment of the truths by which men live. It is for this that He is hailed as the universal man. God's love did not originate at Bethlehem. What began there was its clearest possible expression in the birth of Jesus Christ.

. . .

The Christ of God has commerce with the powers of the universe. By rising from the dead Jesus asserted His dominion not only over the grave but also over the forces in this present life that would keep men from coming to full stature as the sons of God. The visible and invisible structures that influence our existence have been subdued by Christ. This is the thrust of those bracing words that mount to a promontory of hope in Romans 8:

Then what can separate us from the love of Christ? Can affliction or hardship? Can persecution, hunger, nakedness, peril, or the sword? 'We are being done to death for thy sake all day long,' as Scripture says; 'we have been treated like sheep for slaughter'—and yet, in spite of all, overwhelming victory is ours through him who loved us. For I am convinced that there is nothing in death or life, in the realm of spirits or superhuman powers, in the world as it is or the world as it shall be, in the forces of the universe, in heights or depths—nothing in all creation that can separate us from the love of God in Christ Jesus our Lord" (Rom. 8:35-39, NEB).

When the Apostles' Creed affirms that Jesus "ascended into heaven and sitteth at the right hand of God the Father Almighty" it means to say, among other things, that Jesus Christ presides over history. His place is at the headquarters of the universe. Many men, following their death, have had an after-influence. Jesus has more. His is an *after-activity*. Nothing that takes place anywhere is lacking in reference to Him.

To espouse an "area code" theology that would conveniently limit Christ's reign in the present to individual hearts or that enclave of the faithful which we call the church is to undercut a truth of telling magnitude. How can we confine Christ to the narrow precincts of the soul, or to the enclosures that contain His sheep, and still believe that in Him "everything in heaven and on earth was created, not only things visible but also the invisible orders of thrones, sovereignties, authorities, and powers: the whole universe has been created through him and for him. And he exists before everything, and all things are held together in him" (Col. 1:16-17, NEB)?

Kenneth Cauthen's words will help keep us from provincializing Christ: "The Bible opens (logically and factually) with the affirmation that in the beginning God made the heavens and the earth, and it closes (logically and factually) with the affirmation that in the end the whole cosmos will be brought to a glorious fulfillment."[4]

Most Christians believe that Jesus Christ is Lord of their hearts, however broken their obedience. Many are able to see Him as the rightful Lord of the church, however slight the resemblance of the body to its head. All too few of us ever look for Him, much less find Him, in the cross-ruff of current events as the present Lord of history. When Christians hold to a too-small Christ, they lose the ability to resist false sovereignties and tend to make an idol out of family, race, or nation.

I recall my first and only visit to the Pentagon. Like most visitors, I was impressed by the size of this building, a veritable self-contained city, housing some of the most influential personalities of our time. What I remember most, however, is a display set up at one end of the long rectangular plaza. It was put there by the chaplains who serve our Armed Forces. I dubbed it, perhaps irreverently, "God's corner." In view there were the basic symbols of the major faiths: the crucifix, the Star of David, the open Bible. So far so good. But a legend ran above it all: "In a democracy, religion is necessary to the success of national effort." There you have it—God reduced to the level of a means! However worthy the end, the Almighty must never be seen as a means to anything. Such talk suggests that an idolatory of country is at work.

If Christ be in truth the Lord of the world, we make a travesty of His reign by restricting His sovereignty to our individual lives. I have known Christians who were more concerned to find the will of God on the question of whether women should bob their hair than to know the mind of the Eternal on apartheid or overpopulation. A priest who for years had listened to the confessions of nuns was asked what it was like to have such an experience week after week. He replied with a twinkle in his eye, "It's like being stoned to death with popcorn!" When a consideration of Christian ethics begins with questions like mixed bathing, dancing, Sunday movies and the like, the Lordship of Christ is humiliated by caricature. By burrowing into the small questions we can easily miss the large—and in the process, miss our date with destiny.

The world can be forgiven for failing to know and recognize the sovereign rule of Christ. But what defense can Christians offer up for underestimating the jurisdiction of the one they hail as Lord?

Better we should move in the other direction and explore the question of our Lord's connection with other planets now within our ken and reach. His credentials are more awesome than we have ever dared to guess, on our most believing day. As a poet has put it:

> For God has other words for other worlds
> But for this world, the Word of God is Christ.[5]

CHAPTER III

On Taking History Seriously

In the main, Christians in this country have not taken history seriously. We tend either to take a transcendental view of human story, sitting above it all; or regard history as a mere backdrop before which our personal experiences of salvation takes place. Even those ardent Protestants who sit in judgment on the other-worldly features of monastic life are themselves frequently guilty of disavowing the claims of history. The Christ they hear, far from propelling them into serious encounter with the forces that shape men's lives, calls them instead to a private celebration of the love that has done so much for them. They live in a mood of disconnection with their times.

The prevailing view of history in American Protestantism is what might be called the cereal-box view. Those who have ever shopped a supermarket with children will recall that when one gets to the cereal section he buys for what is on the *outside* of the box. The shape and flavor of the contents could hardly matter less. The cutout items on the box are all-determining. Only heaven knows how much cereal has been wolfed down at the breakfast tables of the land in order to hasten the moment when some vaunted prize, puzzle, or coupon could be happily excised.

Such is history to a lamentable number of professing Christians in these United States. It is only a framework within which an elect number of fortunate men and women participate privately in the drama of redemption. It is not the *world* God loves, only a select company of individuals now languishing within it. All the armies that ever marched, all the navies that ever sailed, all the legislative bodies that ever worked to hammer out just laws, all the hopes and fears of tired masses yearning to be free are meaningless. This nonview of history is the Achilles heel of Fundamentalism. It helps explain how Bible-belt country can house at the same time the strongest klaverns of the Ku Klux Klan. At bottom it amounts to a denial of Christ's Lordship over all of life.

Men tend to emigrate from the larger field of history and concentrate on the mini-ventures that comprise their personal story. Their commitment frequently extends no further than to family and career. Personal goals become obsessive. Surrounding events are noticed only when they interfere with the quest for self-aggrandizement. The man whose life lacks public reference usually has no complaint with Providence so long as he can "do his thing."

Christians have an unfortunate way of falling into this same indifference. Their "thing" is getting the gospel out. A country that allows them to do their thing is good, a country that doesn't is bad. It's that simple. Nothing else matters. A while ago I chanced upon a news program on a "Christian" radio station. (I agree with George Buttrick that the term Christian is more safely used as noun than adjective.) We were encouraged to rejoice in the word just released of some minor liberties that had been accorded the evangelical press in Spain. I am as zealous as the next man for seeing the Scriptures printed and disseminated on the widest possible scale. But where has our concern been all these years for the people of Spain, who have suffered one repression of spirit after another under a tyrannical Fascist regime?

Battista's Cuba presents a similar case in point. The island was "good" under this dictatorship because we were permitted to "do our thing." A semblance of religious liberty prevailed. The crushing weight of poverty that kept the little people pinned to a life of unremitting toil troubled us hardly at all. There was scarcely a protest from Christians in this country as affluent members of our society year after year used Cuba for a sugar bowl, a rum pot, an ash tray, and a winter bathing beach. Castro's insurgency aroused us, not because we had a better plan to counter the exploitation he was trying to redress, but because the main-line denominations in this country—not to mention many large corporations—were no longer able to do business as usual under the revolutionary government.

Such an ahistorical interpretation of events is not only dangerously simplistic; it compromises the integrity of the very gospel that we yearn to see enthroned. We have been similarly myopic in our approach to the revolutionary expectations of the people of Africa and other citizens of the Third World.

Arend Th. van Leeuwen in his significant work, *Christianity in World History,* somberly observes that "ninety-nine per cent of people, irrespective of race, play a passive as opposed to a creative role; and even the creative section are passive with regard to ninety-nine per cent of their civilization."[1]

It is to our shame as Christians that these percentages describe us no less accurately than they do other people. And this despite the fact that we claim allegiance to one who has done battle with the powers and freed us for a life of service on behalf of the world He loves!

It is also to our loss. Some of the choicest young people in the nation remain unpledged to the Christian cause because they cannot countenance the church's disengagement from life, or its concentration on matters of minor ethical significance while the world burns. They are of the company of those who will not be told that urban blight, arms control, racial inequities, family planning, conservation of natural resources, etc., are "out of bounds" to their prying minds or unworthy of their passion. Schools of social work in our major universities are crowded with students who got their initial fire-power from a brush with the Gospels, directly or indirectly, only to find that the church did not take its own documents seriously. Many of today's young people have little difficulty believing that God was in Christ. What they find it hard to accept is that Christ is in the church. Their position is succinctly summarized in the epigram, "Jesus, yes—the church, no."

Those who enjoy repartee and curbstone debate cannot help but be drawn to that occasion during Holy Week when Jesus was confronted with the cleverly loaded question, "Is it lawful to pay taxes to Caesar, or not?" (Matt. 22:17). If Jesus answers Yes he will be written off by the Jews as a collaborator. If He answers No he will provoke the wrath of Rome.

Jesus counters by requesting a coin and asking a question of his own: "Whose likeness and inscription is this?" The answer, "Caesar's." The Master goes on, "Render therefore to Caesar the things that are Caesar's, and to God the things that are God's" (Matt. 22:20-21).

This answer closed the conversation and delivered Jesus, for the time, from those who had sought to trip him up. But more, His answer established for His disciples the fact that they had a valid obligation to two realms, the temporal and the eternal, the world of politics and the world of prayer, the order of nature and the order of grace.

A quick turn through the pages of Church history will verify the fact that across the years of the Christian era followers of Christ have shortchanged Caesar at least as much as they have shortchanged God. Protestants, no less than Catholics, can be characterized by a world-denying monastic pull. The glint of heaven in the eye has a way of blinding men to the realities of earth. Faith easily becomes a haven that shelters from involvement rather than a force propelling men to action in the here and now.

Politics then is seen as a dirty business that people of Christian self-esteem assiduously avoid. The sphere that Caesar represents becomes a necessary evil that had best be posted as off limits to the Christian. By thus abdicating the field, a vacuum is created that others neither blush nor hesitate to fill. Frederick William I of Prussia was not hampered by modesty when he asserted, "Salvation is of God. Everything else is my affair." To this boast Christians have whispered an acquiescing Amen.

We reached this sorry pass for at least two basic reasons. First, in a burst of false spirituality we have conveniently forgotten what we owe as Christians to the temporal powers. The New Testament does not spend much ink on the subject of church and state. But we dare not read too much into this relative silence, because much is assumed. That passage in Luke 12 where Jesus refuses to adjudicate a dispute between two brothers over the matter of an inheritance is frequently cited as proof that our Lord was indifferent to legal process and downplayed the need for justice. When Jesus said, "Who made me a judge or divider over you?" (Luke 12:14), he was not implying that the case did not warrant judicial attention, simply that it was not *his* mission to provide it.

St. Paul in his Roman letter reminded the infant church to "be subject to the governing authorities. For there is no authority except from God, and those that exist have been instituted by God" (Rom. 13:1).

The Apostle was conscious of his civil rights and astute enough to know that they were grounded in Roman law. His expansive ministry would have suffered appreciably had he not been able to count on Roman jurisprudence, Roman roads, the Roman postal system, Roman markets, and Roman shipping. These in turn rested on the unspectacular labors of people who had learned to be at home in the coils of bureaucracy and could take red tape in stride. The Roman law to which Paul appealed depended on a judicial system that required courts and magistrates and clerks. The roads he traveled suggest road commissioners, civil engineers, and tax collectors. The mail he circulated implies the existence of postal officials and clearly spelled-out regulations. The ships on which he sailed made him a beneficiary of Rome's maritime safety standards and licensing procedures. His employment as tentmaker made him party to the economic system of the day. The money he earned and raised depended for its worth on the government that issued it. Most of all, he benefited from the *Pax Romana*, with its law and order which suppressed anarchy and made life possible. Surely the gospel in those days would not have made its way into the world at such astonishing speed had each man been allowed to do "what was right in his own eyes" (Judg. 21:25).

Governments are never perfect, and clearly there are times when they become so demonic and corrupt that revolution is the only way out. God plucks up as well as plants. Nonetheless, it is unfair of Christians to underestimate how much they owe the powers that be. In I Peter we read "Be subject for the Lord's sake to every human institution, whether it be to the emperor as supreme, or to governors as sent by him to punish those who do wrong and to praise those who do right" (I Peter 2:13-14). To restrain evil and promote the common good, these are the services the state is here to furnish. When we write politics off as a grubby business and withhold our involvement, save for taxes, we become as those who live at another's expense without making proper return. Sadly the *New York Times* editorialized one day: "We have a great treasury of talent in the city but it is not available for the city."[2]

A second reason why we give practical assent to the two-spheres dictum of Frederick William I of Prussia lies in our demonstrated inability to translate love into justice. In *God's* realm the key word is love. This is the lone absolute of Christian living. "Thou shalt love the Lord thy God with all thy heart, and with all thy soul and with all thy mind. . . . Thou shalt love thy neighbour as thyself" (Matt. 23:37, 39). With those words Jesus summarized the law and set love at the heart of Christian obedience.

In *Caesar's* realm, however, the crucial word is justice. Out there where sovereign states interact with one another and mundane systems operate at corporate levels, we can do no more—nor is more required of us—than to enthrone justice. As Brunner put it, "It is one and the same God who gives us the law of justice by which earthly systems are framed and the law of love for our relations with our fellowmen. For it is one and the same God who established the orders of creation as orders for our time, and gave the promise of the eternal life in which those orders shall pass away."[3]

We do not help matters as Christians by ignoring the distinction between love and justice. I do not want the telephone company to love me. I simply want good service at fair rates. Likewise, the telephone company does not want my love, just a prompt and honest paying of the monthly bill. A federal judge who happens to be enjoying a life of deep and intimate communion with God has no right to sit on the bench and exonerate a criminal just because beneath his robe beats a heart that is charged with a lively sense of the unmerited grace of God. In his representative capacity as one who upholds and administers law for the people of the land he must mete out justice. Should he feel led to do something helpful for the defendant he is forced to sentence, he will do this after hours as a private citizen and not as a servant of the state.

Society functions at the corporate level on the assumption that we will take what is rightfully ours and pay what we rightfully owe. The sentimentalist who keeps wanting to introduce love at *this* level simply clogs things up. At an intersection with a four-way stop there is an established order for starting up should two or more cars arrive at the same time. A driver who has the right of way and seeks to defer to another, possibly because his soul is diffused with love that day, fouls up the system and could conceivably cause an accident. It is assumed that a football team will accept or decline a penalty purely on the basis of self-interest. Can you imagine a team captain saying, "I think we'll refuse the penalty. It would hurt the other team to have fifteen yards walked off against them now"?

Caesar's realm involves us in those thorny questions of how an individual relates to corporate entities and how corporate entities relate to individual men and women. There are people who claim to be Christians who would not think of scampering off with a dollar bill that happened to fall from a woman's handbag, but who would gladly bilk the gas company out of twenty or thirty dollars if given half a chance. Talk to insurance claims adjusters and learn how otherwise upright citizens turn into predatory fighters when they have a chance to "hang one on the company" by inflating claims and indulging in plain dishonesty. Those motorists who toss slugs into toll baskets at bridge and turnpike entrances would probably never think of stealing from another person. A Port Authority or state highway department is fair game, however, since corporate entities lack soul and exist only as legal bodies created by the state.

And it works the other way, too. There are men and women in this country who claim membership in the Christian church and sit as directors of our large corporations, who think nothing of approving sales and production practices designed to short-change the public. One recalls a major scandal of a decade back in which several corporations were indicted for fixing prices on generator installations at the expense of scores of municipalities across the country. Drugs have been prematurely released by pharmaceutical houses, over the protest of physicians on their staffs, because instant sales would brighten the profit picture. After years of deceptive merchandising practices in this country we are just getting around to a "truth in packaging" bill that means something. In New York City a motorist needs 20-20 vision to read the rate schedule of a parking lot, and a degree from M.I.T. to understand it.

To cite these examples at random is to suggest the double standard that has come to be accepted because we have not worked hard enough to clarify the connection between love at the personal level and the need for just relationships where corporate entities are involved. No amount of love in the man-to-man sector will redeem our faith from the charge of irrelevancy if we treat justice as a minor footnote on the page of history.

Clearly there are two realms that belong to life as we experience it. Each affects the other. A commitment to the separation of church and state cannot be made to mean that there is to be no interaction between the two without damage to both. However real the prospect of heaven to many in the Church, and however brief our three-score years and ten by contrast with eternity, this earth remains the only place open to us now in which to give expression to our faith. Unless our light shines here it doesn't shine at all! And that light at its best will flash two beams—the beams of love and justice. Life at the personal and institutional levels needs the illumination of both.

CHAPTER IV

Two Cheers for Christian Secularity!

Can you imagine the nervous tensions that would be touched off were Congress to decree that henceforth Americans were to *stop* on green and *go* on red? After all these years of doing it the other way! Pedestrians and motorists alike would buckle under the strain. Deeply ingrained habits and conditioned reflexes can be altered only at the cost of pain.

Something like this has been happening to the Christian church of late. Many laymen and not a few ministers are positively bewildered as they find the church apparently reversing itself on one front after another. Once a protector of society's values, the church today is bringing those values into question. Once a promoter of peace, the church is fast becoming an agent of agitation. Once interested exclusively in the souls of men, the church is now expressing concern for man's material well-being too. Once warning its members to shun worldliness, the church is now commending worldliness as belonging to the Christian style of life.

We are living in the time of Christian secularity, and as the

King of Siam put it in the Broadway musical, "It is a puzzle-
ment." But there is much in what is going on today for which
we should be grateful. Let's tranquilize our passions for a
moment, lower the decibel count, and try to have an objective
look.

Man today is taking responsibility for his history. There was
a time when he saw himself as a passive respondent to the forces
of life. In the ancient view man considered himself a part of
nature. Since nature is cyclical, he thought of his life as being
cyclical too. His years did not move forward on a line; they
turned in the fashion of a wheel. He stood in awe of nature.
When he sought to win his sustenance from the soil, he was
careful to make peace with the powers that be through ritual
and sacrifice.

In the medieval view of history, man was still essentially
passive. True, there was a plan now that was associated with the
will of God. A hierarchy of values was thought to exist that
reached its apex in Jesus Christ. But the medieval kingdom of
metaphysical essences made no room for vital personal experience and decision. Man simply accepted his place in life as
belonging to God's will. He did not think to challenge or im-
prove his station.

But today man has historicized everything in his life. He is
not content to simply adapt himself to preestablished orders. All
that he has inherited and all the options that stretch out before
him are history to him. This is what is meant by the statement,
"Man has come of age." Life has been desacralized. Man is
willing now to stand up to life and answer back. William Barrett
puts it succinctly when he says, "Man does not have a fixed
essence that is handed to him ready-made; rather, he makes his
own nature out of his freedom and the historical conditions in
which he is placed. As Ortego y Gasset puts it, 'man has no
nature, only a history.' "[1]

It is in the spirit of this insight that Carlyle Marney speaks thus to the church: "There is no point in our continued praying to the Almighty to save a world he has commissioned *us* to save. The strength is in our hands. The knowledge is in our minds. We lack only the will to be and to do, and for *these* we can pray."[2]

This is the exciting and pervasive fact of our time, that man is now taking responsibility for his history. Rather than view this development with suspicion, Christians should rejoice. For this coming of age, this awakened sense of history, has its roots in the Hebrew-Christian tradition. Men like Friedrich Gogarten, Arend van Leeuwen, Hendrikus Berkhof and others have written convincingly to establish this connection.

For centuries the church gave primary emphasis to the personal character of the work of Christ in the hearts of men. Of late, however, New Testament scholars are increasingly calling our attention to the "cosmic value" of Christ. We are beginning now to follow up on some of those slim, shadowy hints given us by St. Paul.

Notice this description of the resources open to Christians. "They are measured by his strength and the might which he exerted in Christ when he raised him from the dead, when he enthroned him at his right hand in the heavenly realms, far above all government and authority, all power and dominion, and any title of sovereignty that can be named, not only in this age but in the age to come. He put everything in subjection beneath his feet, and appointed him as supreme head to the church, which is his body and as such holds within it the fullness of him who himself receives the entire fullness of God" (Eph. 1:19-23, NEB).

In at least four of his epistles the Apostle Paul speaks in a somewhat veiled way about "the powers" of the universe. Hendrikus Berkhof has given us a very fine study of this term

in a book called *Christ and the Powers*.[3] It is his considered
judgment that these powers over which Jesus Christ has tri-
umphed are the structures and orders so vital to man's life,
invisible forces that affect us all. These powers, while necessary
to man's life, can become demonic and work against God's will
for His creation. Keying on the victory that Jesus Christ
achieved over dominions and thrones and powers, the church is
now eagerly bending to the task of beseeching men and women
to enter into the freedom that Jesus Christ effected.

This is the point of D. T. Niles' statement that "the world
is original and ultimate, not the Church: in the beginning there
is earth and a man, and at the end 'there was no temple therein.'
The world isn't here to join the Church, that is an impossible
anachronism. The Church is here to join the world. The world
doesn't owe the Church a living; the Church owes the world its
own true life as world."[4]

What is happening at a breath-taking rate right before our
eyes these days, is that the church is belatedly giving strenuous
attention to humanizing life. We are beginning for the first
time in the Christian era to take history seriously. We are viewing history as something more than a vale of soul-making and
starting at last to move out of our stained-glass foxholes. We
are finally showing as much concern for the public course of
history as for the private course of our individual pilgrimages.
We are at last ready to break camp—to address ourselves to the
very world that is the object of God's love. We are coming to
see that the *good news* in our time is best communicated when
it becomes *hard* news. That is to say, the gospel in which we
believe is most convincing when it gets off the church page and
finds its way into the pages that report on man's ongoing life.
The Lord's Week has become as important as the Lord's Day.

To come at it another way, it would be fair to say that the
church now, perhaps for the first time, is practising the steward-

ship of power. We are coming to see that our reluctance to speak out in the past served to establish the rights and privileges of the haves.

Perhaps it is an oversimplification to look at it this way, but there is a sense in which man has been involved in an all-out game of King of the Hill. You remember from childhood how the game goes. The strongest bulls and fights his way to the top and then prepares to defend his position against the renewed assaults of those whom he has beaten. In our country in particular, and in the Western world in general, some who have clutched and scrounged and elbowed and fought their way to the summit have sought to don the striped shirt of the referee and blow the whistle that would signal the end of the game and freeze all positions.

The church, by its insistence that men play the game according to the rules, has worked—unintentionally perhaps—to secure and legitimatize the holdings of the kings at the top. In the spirit of the day, we are now questioning the rules in the interest of justice and fair play. The arrangements under which we live have a history. They are not above review or beyond revision.

This is the kind of worldliness that is pervading the church today, to the consternation of many. We are not interested in collecting Christians out of the world for the church. We are not concerned any longer to incarcerate the layman within the church. We want to share with our people an experience of worship and a knowledge of the faith, then "loose them and let them go" into the world where they belong.

It used to grieve me in one of my earlier parishes that a very distinguished judge who was a member of that church did not avail himself of the midweek opportunities of the congregation. (We ministers, if not careful, tend to run little loyalty checks, and this man had not come out too well.) But one day common sense broke on my poor mind and it occurred to me that it was enough that this man identified himself with the church at worship. I came to see that it was tantamount to a sin against the very world God loves to try to draw him into the church away from his sphere of influence in the interest of a supper or some other midweek activity.

During a Session meeting of a Presbyterian church in the Northwest recently, an elder arose and asked to be excused. He was a member of the city council and had to leave to vote on a matter that was vital to the public-school system. The moderator, of course, granted his request. As the gentleman made his way to the door, one of his fellow elders said, "I hope that education bill passes." The man turned and said, "I didn't know you cared." For the first time ever, that Session began a discussion about an issue that had to do with something other than the immediate life of the church. I contend that that elder went from the Session meeting to the council meeting without ever having left the church!

"Two Cheers for Christian Secularity!" Two cheers but not three. Why do we withhold that vital third cheer that would make endorsement complete? For the simple reason that Christian secularity is not an unmixed blessing. For one thing, the *source* and *center* of man's freedom from the powers is more frequently assumed than proclaimed. It is more than jealousy that prompts me to complain. I learned a long time ago that the world for centuries has been illumined by indirect lighting. Revolutionary movements are not usually courteous. They seldom write thank-you notes to those who have readied history for their coming.

My concern stems from the fact that unless we know the source of our liberation we will fall into the clutches of one autonomy or another. This is precisely the somber note that Berkhof sounds in his study. He writes, "Wherever the missionary endeavour has gone, the curious situation arises that a whole nation gratefully eats of the fruit, but only a minority desires the tree which produced the fruit."[5]

And then, speaking about the difficulty that we encounter as Westerners when we try to export our way of life to the so-called darkened areas of the world, Berkhof says,

Europe and America now flood these areas with all the products of a Christian and anti-Christian secularization. And these are grafted on what are still primarily naturalistic, tribal forms. But the tree, on which these fruits organically belong, is hardly transplanted at all. This means that the people who come in contact with the results of our culture are uprooted by it. The positive background—confrontation with the new Lord—is lacking. The help offered by the West presupposes an appreciation for labour, history and nature, for which there is hardly room, for instance, in the acosmic philosophies of Hinduism and Buddhism.[6]

If we would rightly know the freedom that St. Paul proclaims in that thrilling passage in Romans 8, need we not also know the agony of sin and the release of faith he talks about in Romans 1-7? The gift without the giver is not only bare, it can be dangerous as well.

One is also concerned about secularity because those who take to themselves the task of reshaping history do not always recognize the need for norms and judgment other than their own. Already there is a fundamentalism of the new left. It is dangerous business trying to identify the will of God and pinpoint what He wants done. The best of our aims and methods need some upward reference.

This is what Dr. John Bennett had in mind when he addressed the graduating seniors at Princeton Seminary and noted that "there is much to be said for the celebration of the secular: . . . this emphasis upon [allowing] the creative human enterprises to be themselves, free from ecclesiastical or traditional religious controls. . . . I see, however, a tendency to celebrate the secular in such a way as to allow too much of what goes on under this name to remain without Christian criticism."[7]

Moreover, in trying to rectify the imbalance of many years by emphasizing the social implications of the gospel over the personal, the church is neglecting its mandate to share the good news with all people. These are hard days for every Department of Evangelism in the major denominations. The mood of the day seems to favor saving the world *from the outside in.* But is it not clear that there must be at least a nucleus of men and women in the world who are avowedly loyal to Jesus Christ and consciously intent upon leavening the loaf?

Perhaps we are settling for changes in the systems because we are not radical enough to press for a change in man. It was no less a figure than Nicolas Berdyaev who said,

When people tell me that a "new order" is to be brought about and man is to be released by a change in the mechanism of society, I want to say to them: for God's sake refresh your memory! Your new order is as old as any other. There has never been a time when man was freed by society: he was always at its mercy, at its secular or religious mercy. So it was among the primitive tribes, so it has been ever since and, no doubt, so it will be until the end. A new "order" will arise on the ashes of all orders and as a result of the only effective, the personalistic revolution.[8]

For better or for worse we live in the midst of revolution. It is not our option to stop it, but it is our privilege to participate in it, to help shape and direct it. The question then is whether we are going to retreat into the church to enjoy the comfort of our fellowship and the strength of our creed, or whether we will venture out into the world to work in and for the very earth that Jesus came to save? This is the challenge that comes to us through the poet Ursula Solek, when she writes:

What, finally, shall we say
In the last moment
When we will be confronted
By the Unimaginable,
The One
Who could not be measured
Or contained
In space or time,
Who was Love
Unlimited?

What shall we answer
When the question is asked
About our undeeds
Committed
In his name—
In the name of him
For whose sake we promised
To have courage,
To abandon everything?

Shall we say
That we didn't know—
That we couldn't hear the clatter
Of hearts breaking—
Millions of them—
In lonely rooms, in alleys and prisons
And in bars?

Shall we explain
That we thought it mattered
That buildings were constructed
And maintained
In his honor—
That we were occupied
With the arrangements

Of hymns and prayers
And the proper, the responsible way
Of doing things?

Shall we tell him
That we had to take care
Of the orderly definition of dogmas
So that there was no time
To listen to the sobbing
Of little ones
Huddled in corners,
Or the silent despair
Of those already beyond sobbing?

Or shall we say this, too:
That we were afraid—
That we were keeping busy with all this
To avoid confrontation
With the reality of his meaning
Which would lead us to repentance—
That it was fear which kept us
Hiding in church pews
And in important boards and committees
When he went by?[9]

CHAPTER V

The Conversion-First Hangup

It is one of the comforting illusions of conservative Christians that, if enough people were converted to Jesus Christ, the massive social, political, and economic problems that threaten to undo the world would be speedily resolved. The flip side of this conviction is that until men are converted in sufficient numbers there is little point in working on the issues that clamor for attention.

As I have stated in the Preface, I believe with all the intensity of my being that men can be radically changed wherever the gospel is faithfully proclaimed and honestly received. Love is the most potent force for change we know. And when that love is the divine love for men that visits us in Jesus Christ there is no way of conceiving all it may achieve. The pages of Christian history are crowded with an inspiring array of testimonies to the life-changing power of the gospel. In a day when so many are working to save society from *without,* we dare not lose confidence in the power of Christ to change men from *within.*

This once said however, it does not follow at all, either that a sufficient number of genuinely awakened Christians would make our vexing corporate problems disappear, or that until this number is reached we have no warrant for participating in the agonies of history. Will Herberg sums the matter up clearly when he writes: "Because of its origins in frontier religion American Protestantism was almost from the beginning geared to an individualistic piety, in which right living by the individual was stressed, with the expectation that social justice would naturally follow."[1]

The fact of the matter is that in those states or communities that are blessed with a high concentration of Christians the claims of justice are as flagrantly unheeded as they are in less "favored" places. Let it be remembered that a Christian nation dropped the first atomic bomb. It is a Christian regime in South Africa that perpetrates the evils of apartheid. It was the Christian West that sat by quietly while six million Jews were incinerated in Nazi ovens. It is the lily-white, predominantly Christian suburb in the north that effectively shuts the black man out. It is the quiet Christian southern town that keeps the black man "in his place." Christians are not conspicuous for their capacity to reckon seriously with justice.

Moreover, a disclaimer must be filed against the view that until we have a goodly number of believers on hand (the percentage is never even approximately defined) we have no business trying to effect justice anywhere. Surely there can be elemental justice with or without a Christian plurality. It is arrogance to think otherwise, and very much against the facts of experience.

New York City could hardly be called a Christian metropolis. Yet basic justice prevails in such day-to-day operations as traffic flow, access to parks, garbage collection, mail delivery, police protection, etc. One is not saying that in these or similar areas of the city's life full justice has been achieved. The point is that at least a working form of justice has been established, despite the fact that fully awakened Christians are a minority. This truth is so obvious that to argue further would be to tax the reader's patience.

The flawed assumption behind the notion that, the more converted people we have on the premises, the better the chance for justice, is the belief that an experience of Jesus Christ automatically endows one with a knowledge of what is right and wrong in complicated matters of corporate justice. Sad to say, this is not the case.

Justice is not that simple. It involves the weighing of rival claims. It is tied in part to political and social reality. Years ago Aristotle enumerated four kinds of justice, and his analysis is still valid. As you scan the list, ask yourself, if you are a believing Christian, what peculiar wisdom you have in any of these categories *because of your faith.*

1. Commutative justice—having to do with *one-to-one* obligations—as in buying and selling and entering into contract with another.

2. Distributive justice—having to do with *the many to the one*—as in the way a political state cares for the poor or pensions its employees.

3. Contributive justice—having to do with *the one to the many*—as in the way an individual pays his taxes or a club member his dues.

4. Corporate justice—having to do with *the many to the many*—as in union-management agreements and trade treaties between sovereign political states.

Honesty compels the admission that Christians do not qualify as experts in any of these areas just because they are Christians. Competence in these fields is not an automatic reflex of religious experience. A Christian may go on to study law and become a distinguished jurist, but in such a case he would be qualified by professional training and not by personal faith alone.

Let's come at this same conclusion down a different runway. Imagine for a moment that the town in which you live has become totally Christian. Every last soul in that community is committed without reservation to Jesus Christ and owns no higher loyalty than his loyalty to the will of God. How would those saintly citizens respond to, say, the question of where a new four-lane bypass should be located? Whose farm will be clipped? Whose sleep will be disturbed by the incessant hum of highway traffic? Who should be allowed to make a killing on the sale of land?

What would a fair sign ordinance look like in that community? What would be a just wage for members of the police and fire departments? If there is a university in the town, what would be a desirable balance between undergraduate and graduate students in the overall enrollment?

At the national level, if we were to project a country in which every citizen was a keenly dedicated Christian what would an equitable draft law look like—or would there be one at all? How steep would the incline be in a graduated income tax? What would a farm subsidy bill look like? How would a balance be established between the claims of society and the rights of individuals before the law?

On the growing edges of our life together in this jet-propelled century, questions confront us that never troubled our fathers. At what point in the testing process should a pharmaceutical house be allowed to release a drug for public use? Does the state have the right to propagandize on behalf of "the pill"? Should the federal government give budget priority to a moon shot or urban renewal? Should homosexual intimacies between consenting individuals be regarded as violations of criminal law? When is a person really dead (a question doctors wrestle with in a day when hearts can be surgically transplanted)?

Enough has been said to rout once and for all the illusion that a converted person will know what to say to all these questions just because he lives in touch with God. His intimacy with the Almighty should make him a concerned and willing learner, but it will not establish him as infallible guide or expert.

Even should the man of faith know what the just thing is in some urgent public matter, he would not necessarily know how to effect that justice or bring the right to birth. Something more is needed than feelings of good will and heated exhortation. Political savvy helps, and some understanding of the dynamics of change in a democratic society.

Justice may be brought about in many different ways. The round table can achieve it—as when a strike is mediated to a satisfactory conclusion. Legislation can achieve it—as in the minimal justice afforded the American Indian by federal law. Economic boycotts can be effective—as in the case of the celebrated bus boycott in Montgomery, Alabama that touched off the modern civil rights movement. At times the ballot box will do it. The schools of Arlington County, Virginia were integrated without a shot being fired, because enough people worked to get an old slate of political leaders out and a new slate in. At times community information programs will get the job done as they bring injustices to light and reduce the fear of change. In many cases demonstrations—the language of the unheard— will accomplish the desired end.

An experience of the grace of God will change the weather of a man's soul and surely make him a better person and a more desirable citizen, but it will not qualify him to know what justice is or how it can be achieved. It is simplistic to a fault to suggest that, were enough people converted, earth's wrongs would be speedily redressed. It is parasitical to remain uninvolved in the large issues of the day while waiting for enough Christians to emerge to constitute a quorum. Surely we are capable of a worthier response than this to the God who said, "Keep justice, and do righteousness, for soon my salvation will come, and my deliverance be revealed" (Isa. 56:1).

CHAPTER VI

Structures, Too, Can Hurt

Do men make the times or do the times make men? This one has divided the house for years and there is no likelihood that we will ever see the question finally put to rest. It was Thomas Carlyle's view of history that man's years on earth can be gathered up in the biographies of the towering personalities that shaped each generation. Others would maintain that there are forces loose in the world in every age before which man is little more than a respondent.

It is not copping out to suggest that a both/and resolution is in order here. Something in us recoils from the philosophy that man is essentially passive before the onslaught of the events that comprise his years. To suggest that man is inert, like a piece of chewing gum rolling around in the jaws of history, is to make a travesty of freedom and bid accountability be gone.

There are some "givens" in life that come to us without our willing. Our time on history's darkling plain is assigned us, as is our place. I had no choice this morning as to whether I would don a coat of mail, saddle a horse, and attempt to rescue the king's daughter from an enemy fortress. The time and place I fill preclude such daring, assuming I had the inclination, but open doors on options at least equally exciting.

Our sex is assigned. Each of us is born to a blue blanket or a pink—and no one thought to ask us which we wanted. Our bodies tend to brittleness or strength—and these we did not choose. Each individual is differently endowed as to psyche, cast of personality, emotional timbre, and skill of mind or hand. Is it any wonder that in the grip of galling disappointment men have been known to curse the powers that be and cry to heaven, "Why has thou made me thus?"

The Christian church, of course, from the beginning has been aware of the interplay between divine Providence and human freedom. It has appealed to men to stop whimpering about the uncontrollable and get on with the business of building a life acceptable to God and useful to the world. The gambler is not responsible for the hand that is dealt him, but he is for how he plays it. The composer must submit to the autonomy of *meter*, 3/4, 2/4, 6/8, but within that fixedness he reveals himself in the *rhythm* that he fashions.

Perhaps the key word in the last paragraph is "uncontrollable." We are not as certain as our fathers that man is more free than conditioned. R. E. C. Browne offers a penetrating two-pronged definition of sin as "the refusal to control what can be controlled and the attempt to control what cannot be controlled."[1] It would be fair to say that under the relentless pressures emanating from such disciplines as psychiatry, sociology, and genetics, the area of the controllable has shrunk. A man's ancestors reach him through his genes. Environmental factors can stretch him tall or shrink him to a whisper of the self he might have been.

This is why we hear so much these days about the need for altering the structures of society. Structures are nothing more than the arrangements under which men carry on their life together. They have to do with who lives where, how taxes are levied, whose sons get drafted, the quality and availability of public education, the wages that prevail, who can vote, the degree of welfare provided for the needy. The structures that a society establishes or permits profoundly influence its citizens. This we are coming to see more and more.

It is the glib assumption of the self-made man that he got where he is on his own (with an odd prayer here and there to the god of success), and that society's nonachievers could get there too if only they would get off their assorted duffs and begin to apply themselves. He is mistaken on both counts.

First, he did not make it entirely on his own. Leaving out such obvious factors as heredity and health, it is sufficient to quash his case to point out that the system in which he operates was indispensable to his triumphs. How far would his get-up-and-go have taken him had he been born in China? Whose rickshaw would he be pulling now? What would his estate be worth had he come into the world with a black skin to work the copper mines in South Africa? How high would his star have soared had he been born in this country on an Indian reservation?

Second, to assume that the less fortunate could rise up and evict their apathy by an act of will underestimates the debilitating down-drag of such depressants as economic privation and racial discrimination. The brown taste of poverty does something to a man. White racism inflicted systematically on blacks collapses ambition and erodes incentive. This is not to idealize the have-nots and villainize the haves. It is simply a way of getting at the point that the structures under which we live have sharp bearing on the kind of men we are. They are not just "there" as so much neutral scenery.

What's more, we are coming to see with merciless clarity that structures can be changed. They are not the divinely ordained, sacrosanct, inviolate arrangements we had thought. They have been assembled by man and thus can be altered, destroyed, remade, or buttressed by man as well. One of the startling new facts of our time is that man on this desacralized planet is taking responsibility for his history. This is the gold that gleams in the ore of secular Christianity. (And one can value the insight without having to go on to jauntily declare the death of God.) Man is not rolling over and playing dead before the powers and orders of a civilization that has been so inattentive to the hungry, the thirsty, the sick, the imprisoned, and the disenfranchised. In the light of Browne's definition of sin, alluded to above, it could be said that man is no longer refusing to control what can be controlled.

Why must the church be so slow coming over to the right side here? At our worst we have baptized prevailing structures. Witness Fundamentalism's indefensible insistence through the years that discrimination against blacks can be justified on the grounds that God cursed the sons of Ham. (Actually Noah did it, and he was drunk at the time!) At best our silence and non-involvement have deprived the voiceless and powerless of our advocacy and influence. Our preachments too often assume that sin resides exclusively in men. When will we see and really believe the companion truth that evil lurks in systems too, and that God is concerned about both!

By putting all our money on the principle of solitary ethical action we remain inept and naïve in a world where we are supposed to manifest the wisdom of serpents as well as the harmlessness of doves (Matt. 10:16). How long must we be saddled with an ethical vision that can see nothing better than a host of individual Christians going about like so many half-sanctified Lone Rangers performing works of mercy here and there? Is our ministry to center exclusively in caring for the casualties spawned by unjust systems, or are we to address our vast resources of till and spirit to bettering the systems also? A

·

guard rail at the mountain's peak can be more effective than a
siren-throated ambulance cavorting at the bottom.

Actually, our personal works of mercy (love) lose their capacity to glorify God when performed within imperfect systems
which we have the power to change (justice). This is the moral
tragedy of the antebellum South. There is no reason to doubt
that many slaveholders, perhaps most, were kind to the slaves
they owned. Slaves represented sizable economic investments,
and it is the better part of prudence to take care of one's investments. Besides, many owners lived in conscious commitment to
the Scriptures and wanted for religious reasons to do the con-
siderate and decent thing. The Master would, indeed, drive his
team through blinding rain in the dead of night to get medicine
for an ailing slave. The Lady of the plantation would see to it
that Mammy got the best of care when travail came upon her.
But all such deeds, however noble their inspiration and unal-
loyed their motive, lost whatever efficacy they might have had
because they were performed within the context of glaringly
unjust arrangements that did not have to be!

The little man in our society has struck his tents and is on
the march. He seeks not patronage but power. He will no longer
remain a docile recipient of our unpredictable benefactions. He
craves justice more than kindness. He wants swift possession of
the right to work, the right to belong, the right to learn, the
right to own, the right to reside, and the right to vote.

The question before the house is whether as Christians we
will help change the structures on behalf of those who stand
on the outside looking in, or disdain this kind of fight and
continue to concentrate on personal acts of kindness and social
service. In all likelihood the man who was mugged on the road
from Jerusalem to Jericho did not know that the priest and the
Levite passed him by as he lay there dazed and hurt. With us
it's different. The poor, the segregated, the hurting members of

society have wit enough to know when help is given and when it is withheld. The priest and Levite (religious types) doubtless justified their going by on the other side by asking, "What will happen to *me* if I stop?" A more fitting question would have been, "What will happen to *him* if I don't?"

CHAPTER VII

The Silence of the
New Testament

Aboard a jet one day I chanced to strike up a conversation with a man who was obviously concerned about the church's involvement in what he called secular issues. He was worried that the church had gone too far, I that the church had not gone far enough. Since each was to remain anonymous to the other there was no need for deferential niceties or tiptoe talk.

This man who shared a center arm rest with me, and probably 90 per cent of my convictions about the Christian faith, based his appeal for the church's withdrawal from controversial social, political, and economic issues on the allegation that the New Testament gives us no mandate for going at things that way. This position is widely and sincerely held and deserves a serious response.

It must be conceded that the New Testament, for the most part, deals with what might properly be called "solitary ethical action." Paul's admonitions have to do almost entirely with one-to-one relationships. A quick look at the closing section of each of his epistles will bear this out. Where the matter under treatment goes beyond one-to-one relationships it usually has to do with a Christian's attitude and behavior toward his fellow believers, not toward the raging issues of the day.

One must further concede that in the one big opportunity St. Paul had to rally the church against the institutionalized evil of slavery he did not come through. His letter to Philemon regarding Onesimus, the fugitive slave, is simply one Christian winsomely appealing to another to receive a penitent servant back without punishment. Paul did not use the occasion to launch a crusade, militant or otherwise, against slavery as such. The New Testament is similarly reticent on other corporate abuses such as gladiatorial games, the subjugation of woman, the militant rule of Rome, and a tax system that placed intolerable burdens on the poor of conquered nations.

A case almost as strong can be made for the four Gospels in general and the teaching of Jesus in particular. To see Jesus as a political or social reformer is to see what really is not there. Time and again he withstood the crowds who implored him to lead out against Rome. He rejected the Zealot option with no less vigor than he showed in refusing to throw in with the collaborationists.

The thrust of Jesus' teaching was to bolster men on an individual basis against pressures from without and stresses from within. Men were to pray and not faint (Luke 18:1); to forgive and not avenge (Matt. 18:35); to trust and not be anxious (Matt. 6:25-34); to believe and not doubt (John 20:27). He resisted the invitation to adjudicate a dispute between two brothers (Luke 12:14), and consistently made it clear that His kingdom was not of this world.

It would seem on the strength of such considerations—and each could be amplified further—that one might safely conclude that the Christian church has no business moving as a corporate entity into such areas as race relations, war and peace, poverty, hunger, population control, conservation, etc.

But such a conclusion lacks credibility in the light of other factors that must be reckoned with. First, the church is rooted in the Scriptures of both the Old and New Testaments. A chap by the name of Marcion took cleaver in hand to trim the Bible to suit his fancy and was branded a heretic by the Roman Church in 144 A.D. Without so much as a half-hesitation he had lopped off the thirty-nine books of the Old Testament. Not bad for openers. Marcion is no longer with us, but his tribe lives on. It is astounding how many Christians one meets who regard the Old Testament as expendable, or reduce it to a happy hunting ground for proof texts that are thought to enhance the credentials of the Christ.

The failure of the church to grapple seriously with corporate responsibility and lead her people beyond personal morality rises in large part from a failure to take the Old Testament seriously. The Hebrews knew the importance of personal trust and individual responsibility, but they knew as well that the Community of Faith had a responsibility to see that justice was established in the land.

Justice in Israel was to be continually tested by looking to the condition of the orphan, the widow, and the stranger. Those three terms toll like a mighty carillon through the Old Testament documents. Each represented a claim of helplessness on the conscience of the state. The strong and the wealthy were not to forget the casualties of a system that had been good to them, or those who had been victimized by an errant toss from Providence. The power of prophets like II Isaiah and Amos can be most keenly felt when one catches the peal of the thunder they unleashed against the rich for their abuse of the poor (e.g., Isaiah 58, Amos 3). To totally privatize biblical religion one would have to find a way to erase such voices from the tape.

When it comes to the four Gospels and the teachings of Jesus, a more careful reading will reveal that there is more that is radical here than we might wish would be the case. We have a way of hearing and retaining what is congenial to our station. The "Magnificat" that Mary sang as she carried the Savior in her womb can hardly fail to rouse us with its strident revolutionary tone, even when we read it in the shockproof language of the King James Version. The passage Jesus chose to read in the synagogue at Nazareth as he began his public ministry might well be viewed as the job description he accepted for himself. It is not unlike the song of Mary, that quotation from Isaiah 61. It speaks of good news being preached to the poor, of release, of recovery of sight and of liberty (Luke 4:18).

While Jesus' peculiar vocation was that of the Suffering Servant sent to give His life for the redemption of the world, and while it may be true that He anticipated but a short interval between the close of His earthly ministry and the coming of God's kingdom, it belongs to the picture to recognize that Jesus was seen as a perennial threat by those who represented the religious and political establishment of the day. The Pharisees and Sadducees, long opposed to each other, saw in Jesus such cause for alarm that they closed ranks against Him. The House of Herod honored Him with worry from Bethlehem to Golgotha. Pilate seemed unsteady in the trial that pitted him against the Galilean even though he had the force of Rome behind him.

However eschatological Jesus' ethic might be deemed to be, He did focus the attention of His followers with tensor lamp intensity on the needs of this world. The neighbor in want must be ministered to. Correctness of theology is secondary. Ultimate judgment will be meted out on the basis of food given to the hungry, drink shared with the thirsty, visits made to the imprisoned, compassion shown to the sick, hospitality showered on a stranger (Matt. 25:34-40). True, one cannot wring from this parable of the Great Assize stimulation for more than the expression of man-to-man care on a personal basis. But this may be due more to political wisdom on Jesus' part than to a reluctance to see His followers tackle human problems at an organized level.

It would have been premature to the point of folly to have those first believers attempt a run at any of the built-in evils of the Roman Empire. It is blindness on our part, however, that keeps us from seeing that our present is ripe with opportunity to strike some needed blows at wrongs too long ignored.

The prayer in which all Christians gladly share will not let us forget the importance of what we should be doing here and now: "Thy will be done in earth even as it is in heaven."

In this same vein, when we scan the letters of St. Paul and conclude that the early Christians *did not* set out to right social, political, and economic wrongs, we would be better advised to say that they *could not*. They were a tiny minority in a sprawling empire, almost totally lacking in the power so necessary to effect corporate change. To make matters worse, a majority of this minority were slaves, perhaps as many as 75 per cent. They were not their own. They did not possess the right to vote, the right to hold public office, the ability to command large sums of money. It would have been suicidal for the infant church to take on, say, the inferior status of women in the Roman Empire, or the institution of slavery. Aside from a few rumbles recorded in the Book of Acts they abstained from such activity, waiting for the time, should the Lord tarry, when their efforts had a chance to succeed. The inactivity of the New Testament church on this level is traceable more to pragmatic considerations than theological objections. It would be fair to say that it never occurred to Paul to ask how society should be conducted or culture adjusted if Christians should begin to have a voice in such matters.

Those who regard the New Testament church as normative for us on this point seem not to notice that our situation vis-à-vis these United States is altogether different from the situation in which, say, the Colossian or Philippian Christians found themselves vis-à-vis Rome. They lived *under* power while we live *in* power and *with* power. Some 62-65 per cent of the population of this country is formally identified with the Hebrew-Christian tradition. We cannot ask aloud, "What are they doing in Washington?" for *we* are the they! We have the numbers, the wealth, the influence, the power, to make a telling difference. We have a responsibility under God, therefore, to make that difference.

As part of the majority we can no longer enjoy freedom from responsibility for the structures of the nation. The Christian churches of this country have power enough and to spare. We have the power that comes with awarding contracts and purchasing supplies on the open market, the power of influence, the power of numbers, the power that attaches to a reputation for helpfulness. We have the power of prayer and the power of God's mighty Spirit in our midst. Whether we want such power is not up for question. We have it. This is fact. It only remains to be asked whether we will use this power to sanctify the injustices of our society or place it at the disposal of the needy.

Frequently the fear is expressed that the more the church intrudes itself on public life the more vulnerable it will become to the charge of clericalism. A powerful body like the church that begins to flex its muscle will surely find itself a target for resentment. It is further noted, in support of this fear, that Jesus did not assert Himself or throw His weight around.

The Christian church in this country would indeed be guilty

of a misuse of power if it expended its resources on its own
behalf for the saving of its own life. But that power is not
released abusively when it is expended on behalf of others.
Churches deserve the resentment they churn up when they insist
on baccalaureate services for high school graduates in a plural-
istic society, enjoy tax-free business profits, take property off
the tax rolls in communities all across the country, restrict birth
control information on religious grounds, and censor books and
movies on religious grounds rather than natural law.

But churches will be found faithful to their trust when they
place their considerable powers of money, influence, and persuasion at the disposal of those who have little power of their
own. History lies open to the fact that anticlericalism waxes hot
and strong only when the church identifies with the haves at
the expense of the have-nots. So it was in France and Russia
before their revolutions. So it is today in Spain and South
America.

The passive-resistance stance toward life can be rightly traced
to Jesus. But it must not be forgotten that while He refused
to wield power in His own defense, He was not averse to assert-
ing Himself for the sake of others. He lit into the money-
changers on the Temple porch because they had defiled the
house of prayer. He dressed down the Pharisees for laying impossible burdens on the common man. He identified with the
adulterous woman, protecting her from the stones and accusa-
tions of her self-righteous fellow townsmen.

When one uses power for himself he invites the disrespect
that usually follows. When one exerts his power on behalf of
others he bears a witness to the Christ of whom St. Paul said,
"Though he was rich, yet for your sakes he became poor, so
that by his poverty you might become rich" (II Cor. 8:9).

CHAPTER VIII

Christ Our Contemporary

Mention was made in the last chapter that the New Testament is not altogether normative for Christians today as regards their duty to the world, because the life situation in which they find themselves is quite different from the situation experienced by the saints of the New Testament. This is not to suggest that the needs of the inner man today are unlike the felt needs of folk like Timothy or Dorcas. There is, to be sure, a timeless quality to the divinely inspired word that enables it to "find" men without respect to where they are, or when.

So much has rolled off the presses lately stressing the unprecedented nature of these moon-shot, cybernetic years that we are in danger of constructing a uniqueness myth and believing it. The sins of the flesh clicked off for us by St. Paul in his Galatian letter (immorality, impurity, licentiousness, idolatry, sorcery, enmity, strife, jealousy, anger, selfishness, dissension, party spirit, envy, drunkenness, carousing—cf. 5:19-21) are still the stuff with which our news reports are filled. Likewise, the fruit of the Spirit listed in that same chapter are still the qualities in critically short supply in our frayed society (love, joy, peace, patience, kindness, goodness, faithfulness, gentleness, self-control—5:22-23).

No, in opting for the need to go beyond the New Testament we are thinking only of the Christian's role in society. Certain responsibilities belong to us because of our dominant majority status in the Western world, which the Apostles and their colleagues could not so much as have imagined.

It should not disturb us that this is so. The Bible was never intended to be a ready-reference manual designed to produce stock answers to all our questions at a moment's glance. It is more than a casket of glittering generalities sufficiently broad and diffuse to bridge out from any corner into which man can paint himself. If all the answers were there in a book, then all that would be required of us would be to copy them slavishly and apply them to the best of our ability.

But we are called to be more than copyists. We are called as sons to faith. And faith sees the Scriptures not as a dead letter but a living word. There is wide difference between history and revelation. History records how Moses confronted Aaron at the sight of the golden calf (Exod. 32). Revelation asks: "What is God trying to say to me today through what Moses said to Aaron on that raucous occasion?" What Christ said to the rich young ruler is history (Luke 18). What Christ is trying to say to me through what he said to the rich young ruler is what we mean by revelation. We must search the Scriptures and the manuscripts behind them in quest of the purest text. But Christian faith will not leave the matter there. The God who spoke to others in the context of their times is speaking now to us.

It is a strange doctrine of the Holy Spirit that holds God to have been more vocal at one time than another. Why does our inherent stance so consistently point us away from the present to the past? Max Mueller, back in the last century, gave us the term "henotheism."[1] With that word he described the conviction held by many ancient people (not to mention many moderns) that their God was limited in sovereignty and presence to a particular land. Perhaps we need a word to describe our hang-up. Let me place in nomination the term "chronotheism," the tendency to limit God's self-disclosure to certain privileged eras of the past.

It must be nailed down and defended at all cost that God has spoken to men in a definitive unrepeatable way in Jesus Christ. Writers like Paul and Luke and John have a rightful place within the canon of Scripture because they were, as Karl Barth has described them, "primary witnesses" to God's saving deed in Jesus Christ.[2] They are thus part of the revelation, not simply commentary on it, and as such fully deserving of the church's attention in every generation.

But none of these truths, so precious and indispensable to Christian belief, is jeopardized when the Church asks its members to listen to what the Spirit is saying *now*. The past should not be permitted to mesmerize us. Cherished as the writings of the Reformers are to Protestant belief, and worthy as they are of our continuing study, by what definition of the Spirit's work can it be maintained that God was more articulate in the sixteenth century than He could possibly be now? Conservatively inclined Christians have a way of seeing themselves as defenders of the faith. In reality they are often found defending sixteenth-century theology on the assumption that those particular formulations of doctrine are binding on all subsequent generations.

"Chronotheism" would be no threat could we recover the sense of expectancy that belongs to every generation of Christians on the strength of Jesus' promise that the Holy Spirit will guide us into all truth (John 16:13). Our Lord has yet many things to tell us (John 16:12). Here is the openendedness needed to counterbalance the truth of the finality of Scripture. We are not curators of a manuscript museum, but a company of men and women blessed with the privilege of entering into living dialogue with the ever-present Christ through the written word and the impinging facts of contemporary life. From Jesus' statements regarding the Spirit's ministry to the church one can only deduce that more would be revealed as time went on. To keep this "more" from being exploited and appropriated by those who would impose their "inner light" as truth, we must try the spirits (I John 4:1) by reference to the mind of Christ as disclosed in the Gospels. The center of our faith is forever settled, but the growing edge of the circumference is where God's "new" keeps wanting to break in.

We are not likely to hear what the Spirit is saying to the churches now unless we can learn to experience and understand Christ as our contemporary and extricate Him from the trappings and limitations of first-century Palestine. Alas, for many in the Christian church, Christ is hardly more than a historical figure of revered stature, alive today only in the pages of holy writ and the memory of the faithful. How many times have we heard it said that in moments of ethical indecision a believer can do no better than ask, "What would Jesus do *if he were here*"? Have we so egregiously missed the point of our Lord's ascension—that He who came to make His abode in one time and place is now released from such particularities in order that He might fill all times and places! The question might be put more properly were a Christian to ask, "What does Jesus *who is here* wish to accomplish through me in this situation?"

When we treat Jesus as an historical personage and nothing more, then we must get to Him the way we get to other personalities of the past; namely, through the twin disciplines of history, return and reconstruction. By returning we seek to learn as much as we can of the time and place in which the chosen subject lived. By reconstruction we let imagination envision the subject as he must have been in his own era and locale. Thus, to "know" Thomas Jefferson one would read every document extant that would assist in recreating Jefferson's day. One would visit those places that our third president inhabited over the course of his earthly life. One might even attempt to restore and keep immune to change some period piece—perhaps a home—to aid the imagination in its task.

But we do not so learn Christ! St. Paul put it to us straight when he said, ". . . even though we once regarded Christ from a human point of view, we regard him thus no longer" (II Cor. 5:16). The days of His flesh are not to be written off as inconsequential to faith. One is happy to see that New Testament scholars are commencing to speak again for the basic integrity and reliability of the Gospel narratives. The point is that we can better learn the mind of Christ by being open to His presence than by sifting through the dust of another day!

The Gospels say enough to insure Christ's place in history, but they do not say so much that the need for outreaching faith and risk-taking obedience are canceled. If God wanted us to know Christ by return and reconstruction we might be forgiven the observation that He was mighty careless with the records. The Gospels on the whole are indifferent to details of time and place. We do not know for sure just where Jesus was born, or the precise location of the house in Nazareth in which He was raised. We cannot pinpoint the slopes where He delivered the various fragments that came to form the Sermon on the Mount. We do not know the exact location of Golgotha, nor can we identify a particular tomb and claim it with certainty as the place where His body was laid to rest. Loquacious guides in the Holy Land to the contrary notwithstanding, we do not know with accuracy the fine details of Jesus' earthly life.

There is thus no room for shrines in Christian experience. Since one does not know Jesus after the flesh, one need not feel spiritually deprived for not yet having been to Palestine. Culturally deprived—yes, but not spiritually. A visit to the Holy

Land would doubtless advance one's knowledge of history and geography, but it would not necessarily raise the quality of one's faith. It is by no means demonstrable that every Christian who has visited the Near East perceives the mind of Christ more fully than those who have not gone. Jesus is revealed from faith to faith and understood from obedience to obedience.

But to angle back to the purpose of this book, let it be confessed that anything we can do to keep Jesus incarcerated in the first century A.D. will help shield us against His judging presence in these troublous times. Man's sin and savvy has a better chance to prevail uncontested if he can shuck Jesus off as an itinerant berry-picker who belonged to an agrarian society in a different part of the world twenty centuries ago. What could *that* kind of Christ possibly know about welfare grants, air pollution, ABM systems, or population control?

The claim of the New Testament is that He both lives and reigns. In their hearts the faithful know this to be true. In weaker moments, under the assault of doubt, we tend to cling to the past—remembering His incarnation; or yearn for the future—looking to His coming again and the consummation of history; and forget that He is with us now. There is no situation in which His word is not true, no culture in which His healing, judging presence cannot be discerned. No development in human progress can make Him obsolete. No situation, here or conceivable, can render irrelevant what He came to be and say and do. He is the man for all times, all seasons, and all climates. The props on history's stage may change and the players' costumes suffer alteration with the passing whims of fashion, yet He goes on making known the secrets of the heart, bringing down the mighty from their seats and taking up the burden of the weak.

God is up to something in the world. His will and our freedom are strangely interlaced. The choices that confront us are charged with the currents of eternity. Just as chance and change are now adjudged to be the properties of matter, so in the life we live together there are new turns, open futures, and unguessed possibilities. Christ is working still. Where action and reaction clash, He is there. Where men mistake what they are accustomed to for what they are entitled to, He is there. Where the undersiders of history press and squirm for what their manhood needs, He is there.

When the church refuses to follow her Lord into the busy thoroughfares of history, when she talks of love but fails to press for basic justice, when her message has no focus other than the well-being of individual souls and lacks all public reference, when she refuses to put her power on the line on behalf of the disadvantaged, when she is more concerned to perpetuate and adorn her own life than to lose it for the sake of Christ and the gospel—when all of this happens, as it has, the church not only contributes to the social and economic inequities that provoke to violence, but forsakes her Lord as well.

There is a disheartening scarcity of hymns available to the church that convey a vivid sense of the working Christ and an incomplete creation. One I know and love and recommend (sung to the tune Wareham) comes from the pen of William DeWitt Hyde:

> Creation's Lord, we give thee thanks
> That this thy world is incomplete,
> That battle calls our marshaled ranks,
> That work awaits our hands and feet,
>
> That thou has not yet finished man,
> That we are in the making still,
> As friends who share the Maker's plan,
> As sons who know the Father's will.

Beyond the present sin and shame,
Wrong's bitter, cruel, scorching blight,
We see the beckoning vision flame,
The blessed kingdom of the right.

What though the kingdom long delay,
And still with haughty foes must cope?
It gives us that for which to pray,
A field for toil and faith and hope.[3]

CHAPTER IX

Getting On with It

The difficulties that surround a quest for the knowledge and implementation of justice touched on in Chapter V should not be allowed to paralyze us into a state of inertia. Christians can make a sorely needed contribution to society, provided they rid themselves of certain mind-sets that work to keep them on the sidelines like so many parasitical standers-by.

Christian people tend to think in terms of moral absolutes. We like to believe that some things are eternally right and others eternally wrong. We prefer not to have any truck with "in-betweens." When one meets a man who digs in—to the death—in defense of a right that he feels belongs to the final vision of history, one senses that God is nigh. Albert Schweitzer, clinging tenaciously to his "reverence for life" philosophy in Lambaréné, caused the world to doff its hat in hushed respect.

Unfortunately, in the public sector of history one must grapple more with relativities than absolutes. All Christians would agree that love is an absolute. But how can a city council or the Congress of the United States practice love? Once we get beyond man-to-man relationships we find ourselves in a field where the cause of love must march beneath the banner of justice. Brunner puts it plainly when he notes that "in the world of systems the true disciple of the church cannot give effect to his love except by being just. He remains loving nonetheless, but as long as he is active in the world of systems, his love compels him to be just. Within the world of systems, he must, so to speak, change his love into the current coin of justice, since that alone is legal tender in the world of systems."[1] Justice in turn comes through the successful adjudication of rival bids for power.

Most people in their public and corporate lives seldom see an absolute from the time they leave home in the morning until they return at night. What absolute could one appeal to as mayor of New York City that would help determine what the cost of a subway ride should be? What absolute would we advise a member of the State Department to invoke in deciding under what circumstances to recognize a revolutionary government abroad.

Answers to such questions can be but relatively right at best. But relative or not, such answers are indispensable to man's life on earth. It's this or nothing. This is why politics has been described as the art of the possible. It lives on compromise and adjustment. One group's credit is another group's debit, and justice aims to see that the books are balanced fairly. Politics rides the tricky currents that spin and froth and twist among the grey, half-covered rocks that separate the seas of right and wrong.

Armed with absolutes and somewhat naïvely believing that love is the immediate answer to everything, Christians have shunned serious involvement in political activity *as Christians*. Frequently they have been active as members of a union, a board of realtors, a home improvement association, etc., but seldom as members of the body of Christ. It is easier to stand back and renounce politics as a seamy business unworthy of the efforts of a good man. Sean O'Casey makes this point in *The*

Shadow of a Gunman when he has Davoren say, "A man should always be drunk, Minnie, when he talks politics—it's the only way in which to make them important."[2]

There are preachers in this country who delight in berating public officials for their bad judgment and imperfect decisions, but remain singularly silent when it comes to offering constructive counsel as to how matters might be improved. Such "cheap shots" require no erudition and command no respect. If the church is to have any public reference at all, it must learn to function where relatively right and less-than-perfect decisions are the order of the day. *If we are too good for this we are just plain too good.* "Thy will be done through us, O Lord. If not, Thy will be done through others."

Christians are also hesitant to grapple with political and social issues because they feel that their vocation as believers in Christ preempts their vocation as creatures. *Ordinary men* worry about such temporal matters as war, taxes, welfare rolls, urban housing, etc. *Christian men* are called to groom the inner man and work with every power at their command to circulate a knowledge of the gospel.

Let me confess a personal failing on this very point. During the first ten years of my ordained ministry I was asked at least annually to observe Rogation Sunday. According to denominational headquarters this day was to be used for reminding people of the good earth—the resources of the soil, the miracle of fertility—and of their responsibility to care for the earth and husband its treasure.

Overtures regarding Rogation Sunday annoyed me and left me unconvinced. Just another attempt on the part of a few ecclesiastical bureaucrats to inflict a promotional calendar on the church and divert me from the preaching of the gospel! I say it to my shame that in no church that I have ever served have we observed this day.

To my shame, because the fallacy afoot here is the unjustifiable assumption that once a man has experienced grace he no longer bears responsibility for nature. But the truth is that we have duties as men that our calling as Christians does not cancel but enhance. We read in Genesis that God placed man in the garden and charged him with the work of tilling the ground and keeping it. This charge has not been rescinded. *God wills the continuation of His creation as well as the redemption of men.* We read in Genesis 9:9-11 "Behold, I establish my covenant with you and your descendants after you, and with every living creature that is with you, the birds, the cattle, and every beast of the earth with you, as many as came out of the ark. I establish my covenant with you, that never again shall all flesh be cut off by the waters of a flood, and never again shall there be a flood to destroy the earth."

The Holy Spirit who indwells believers, inducing faith and producing holiness, is none other than the Spirit who on creation's morning brought the world to birth. A knowledge of the grace of God does not logically or theologically lead to a disparagement of the earthy. Christians should be as vitally interested in conservation and environmental sanitation as any other people on earth. Nothing human can be stricken off the agenda of the church without weakening our witness and misrepresenting our religion.

Christians have a unique mandate to declare by life and word the good news that Christ is Lord of all and the Savior of any. But fidelity to this commission, far from excusing us from participating in history, plunges us into the thick of it. This ought we to have done and not left the other undone (Matt. 23:23).

At those points where we work for the general betterment of man we will not have the field to ourselves nor will it be true in most instances that we got there first. Those who have worked on any of the diversified fronts of the civil rights movement will know from experience that Christians have no corner on the passion for justice or any consistently superior wisdom on how best to do the job. We enter the fray as learners joining with others of good will, whatever their theology, in a push for the goal line.

This is not to say that Christians are incapable of making a unique contribution of their own to the cause of human welfare. Believing that Jesus is concerned about the little people of the earth, so easily victimized by the powerful in their rush for status and possessions, the Christian ought to be able to sustain his passion for the needy long after the outright humanist has shot his bolt and left the scene. Men like Bertrand Russell and Norman Thomas are the stellar exceptions who prove the rule that there aren't many old liberals in the world.

Time makes conservatives out of most of us. An inner commitment to Christ should help us counter time and provide us with stamina to stay with a good cause long after the first flush of newness and publicity has cooled. Many started out to run the civil rights race as though it were a hundred-yard dash. When it turned out to be a marathon they began to experience the loneliness of the long-distance runner. One who knows the secret of renewal will be empowered not only to "mount up with wings as eagles" but also to "walk and not faint" (Isa. 40:31). Knowing the radical character of evil and its presence in all men, the Christian will not plunk down the key on the front desk and check out at the first sign of perversity on the part of those who need his help.

Moreover, a Christian should be able to keep the world mindful that the struggle for justice and human welfare must be waged on many fronts. There is one conflict but many battle stations. The one-cause man must not be allowed to decatholicize our concern or confine our backing to the one or two issues that happen to be front and center now. The leper in Thailand, the orphan in Hong Kong, the unemployed miner in Appalachia, the elderly, paying out the rope of time in a cold city flat, the prisoner in his cell, the migrant worker drifting from one make-shift dormitory to another, the illiterate, the hungry—all of these have a claim on the conscience of the world. The modern missionary movement, under such heavy attack today, deserves recognition for attempting work on all these fronts over a long period of time with limited funds. If the constant in our cru-sades and programs is human betterment and not merely some political or social ideology, no area of human deprivation can be deemed more worthy of attention than another.

Finally, on this point, the Christian enters the field of human rights conscious of a responsibility to the perpetrators of evil as well as to the victims. His pity will be touched as much by the plight of the segregationist as by the damaged casualties of segregation. The tenants who suffer at the hands of a greedy slumlord will concern him, but so will the ultimate redemption of the slumlord. The Christian sees justice not as an end in itself but as an indispensable means to the only valid end, the reconciliation of all men to each other and to God.

Another mind-set that tends to immobilize us before the political and social evils of the world is the desire to avoid conflict. This is an understandable desire, but it must give way before the easily demonstrated truth that passive acquiescence usually produces a higher accident rate in the long run than bold measures of positive action projected in Christian love. The sin of "going along," when we could do other, is costly for the church in the sight of God and before the court of world opinion.

Pastor Martin Niemoller's confession carries warning for us all: "In Germany, the Nazis came for the Communists, and I didn't speak up because I was not a Communist. Then they came for the Jews, and I did not speak up because I was not a Jew. Then they came for the Trade Unionists and I didn't speak up because I wasn't a Trade Unionist. Then they came for the Catholics and I was a Protestant so I didn't speak up. Then they came for ME . . . by that time there was no one to speak up for anyone."[8]

Churches are not at liberty to stick with safe and manageable subjects while the world convulses. A church whose unity is threatened by a soundly conceived program of community involvement is a church whose unity is spurious to begin with. Our oneness lies in the Christ to whom we respond, not in a tacit agreement to keep everyone on board while waiting for a conflict-free consensus before attempting anything.

Finally, our hands are frequently tied when we contemplate constructive social action because we keep telling ourselves that we do not know how to go about it. One is amazed at the number of people who loudly disclaim any knowledge of how political power works, but suddenly become politically effective when their own little hot-dog stand is threatened! I recall a community of a dozen or so suburban families who prided themselves on being nonpolitical. Overnight those two-car, split-level families became zealous activists upon the discovery that the quiet one-way street that added so much to their enjoyment of life was to be made two-way by action of the city council. The manner in which they banded together, fired off telegrams to key people, marched on city hall, engaged an attorney, circulated petitions, and raised collective hell was a wonder to behold. The principles of political leverage are not all that strange to us. Did you ever see a motorist tear off for City Hall after getting a parking ticket as the victim of a jammed meter?

For a congregation to discharge this part of its mission traditional patterns and procedures will have to be drastically revised. We need new commitment, to be sure, but we need every bit as much a wiser deployment of the commitment we already have. Isaiah exhorted his hearers to *"learn* to do good" (Isa. 1:17—italics mine). The mere proliferation of the good we know already simply will not do.

As a first step one might suggest that a new self-image is required of the minister. The traditional congregational expectation is that he should be their man in public affairs. This expectation has a subtle way of driving him to work *for* the members *from the front* rather than *with* them *from the middle.* But the mission belongs to the church, not to the man. The pastor's ministry is to the congregation, and the congregation's ministry to the world. The pastor as teacher, preacher, and administrator will aim to equip his people for their ministry. The preacher who chooses to bypass his congregation and assume sole responsibility for community penetration will not only do a poor job of it but at the same time deprive his people of their part in an exciting aspect of the church's witness. Ordination does not make a man ubiquitous. He cannot possibly post himself at every station where his people ought to be. A one-man ministry of flurry is poor substitute for a congregation's ministry in depth.

But how to marshal the resources of the congregation for broad-gauged social action? Perhaps the place to start is with the term "organization" itself. This is not a word calculated to stand us on our feet and get us to singing the Doxology. It doesn't turn us on. All the same, there isn't a church in the land worth its salt that hasn't learned to organize for the work it wants to do. There's a canard making the rounds these days that ought to be spiked and buried: "God does not waste time with committees. When He has a job to do, He usually calls one man." Thank God for stellar individuals who come along from time to time to sound the needed word and point the way. But thank God more for common folk, unheralded and unnamed, by whose labors we are saved between our times of inspiration.

Moses was the peerless leader of the Exodus. But the gains of the Exodus were solidified and conserved because Moses had the humility to listen to the counsel of his father-in-law (of all people), who reprimanded him for trying to be a one-man show. As the record has it, "And when Moses' father-in-law saw all that he did *to* the people, he said, What is this thing that thou doest to the people? why sittest thou thyself alone, and all the people stand by thee from morning unto even? . . . So Moses hearkened to the voice of his father-in-law, . . . And Moses chose able men out of all Israel, and made them heads over the people, rulers of thousands, rulers of hundreds, rulers of fifties, and rulers of tens" (Exod. 18:14, 24, 25—italics mine).

To put it plainly, Moses got himself organized and learned to be an administrator. Jesus chose twelve and later seventy, and sent them out two by two. The first item of business taken by those first believers following the resurrection of their Lord was an administrative matter—electing a successor to Judas. Early in the life of that same company, deacons were elected to administer benevolences. We may laugh at committees and describe them derisively as "companies of the unfit appointed by the unwilling to do the unnecessary," but the fact remains that God's business here on earth is largely dependent on the faithful labors of day-to-day people discharging committee assignments.

The minister, however prophetically inclined, who wishes to shape his congregation around his preaching, and see the community, in turn, influenced by the church, will be found giving major attention to the recruitment and deployment of the ranks. There are priorities to be selected, facts to be dug up, studies to be made, publicity techniques to be developed, and overall strategies to be formulated. The trend is toward short-term, hard-hitting *ad hoc* committees (or "odd hack" as a friend let slip one day). A network of hard-working task forces, led from within, will accomplish more in the long pull in today's kind of world than a few individuals ever could, however dedicated, under the star system. If the towel represents the most unwanted task in the service of God, then its equivalent in the church today may well be committee service on a subcommittee charged with finding out how many children on a given street go to school each morning without an adequate breakfast.

The church in fulfilling its role as teacher over the years has become more adept at talking than listening. To be effective at the community level the church will have to go out humbly and listen to those who "know where it's at." Many laymen on the church's rolls would be tickled to share their know-how on political and social problems, could they be led to believe that the church really cares. Testimony would have to be gleaned from purely secular sources too.

It may prove helpful if we digress here long enough to note the various ways in which the church has sought to respond to the disadvantaged since it first began to try. James made it perfectly clear that words alone would never do. "If a brother or sister is ill-clad and in lack of daily food, and one of you says to them, 'Go in peace, be warmed and filled,' without giving them the things needed for the body, what does it profit? So faith by itself, if it has no works, is dead" (Jas. 2:15-17). Jesus, by teaching and example, brought the poor and needy from the periphery of man's concern and emphatically placed them at the center. The Parable of the Last Judgment (Mat 25) provides a terrifying illustration of just how big earth's little people are with God.

No Christian would seriously question the assertion that faith in Christ and concern for others go hand in hand. *Divisions rise over the question of how that concern should be expressed.* There are three ways basically that have emerged over the course of Christian history. They are not in conflict, and there is surely no reason why all should not be operative at the same time.

Historically, God's people first ministered to the "little ones of earth" by extending help on a personal, one-to-one basis. They gave themselves to what Wordsworth once described as "those little nameless unremembered acts of kindness and of love." Outsiders said of those earliest Christians, "Behold how they love one another." There is more of this personal attentiveness in any parish than meets the eye. Sometime I should like to preach a sermon on "The Church the World Can't See." As I make my pastoral rounds I find more times than not that my people have already been there before me—in that depressing home for the aged, in that sickroom, in that hospital, in that apartment where death has recently come. Beneath the surface of any parish there is this network of mutual concern. No matter how society is structured, such kindness will never be obsolete.

The second way by which the church has sought to minister to God's little ones might be described as the way of organized benevolence. Many of man's needs are repetitive. Accordingly we have established, particularly in the Christian world, welfare agencies and service organizations. One girl comes to Chicago from the farmlands, and it is possible to relate her to a family in the big city. When a thousand girls come from farm country to the city in one month, you get the YWCA! One boy wishes an introduction to the disciplines of self-reliance and the wonders of the out-of-doors. A man bends to the task and becomes a father to his son. When dozens of boys in a given community desire this experience you get the Boy Scouts of America. We find across this land—and indeed across the world—an elaborate system of organizations carefully built to express the good will and extend the helpfulness of the community. It is here that we find our homes for the aged, our schools for orphans, our day nurseries, our hospitals, our halfway houses, and a host of others. The Christian conscience, sensitized by Jesus, has coupled this sensitivity with organizational know-how so that needed help might be rendered dependable, uniform, and constant. When care is taken to maintain the personal touch, the spirit of Jesus Christ comes through in these organized expressions of concern. United Funds across the country are examples par excellence.

But there is a third way in which Christian people have sought to minister to God's little people. This is by attempting to change the structures that produce the hungry, the thirsty, the stranger, the naked, the sick, and the imprisoned.

Imagine that next summer, as you drive toward your vacation haunt, you overtake a loosely slatted truck in which are herded a tightly packed company of poor and unkempt people. Presently it dawns on you that these are migrant workers being carted to pick potatoes on Long Island or grapes in Michigan or California. As you make your way to your vacation cottage your conscience begins to gnaw away at you. Here you are in this comfort while just on the other side of the road are these people forced to live in huts unfit for human habitation, and paid a pittance. Your conscience nags you to the point where you wish to do something. You decide initially to do something on a warm and personal basis, so you buy some candy and a few games, go over to the migrant workers' camp, and befriend a child or two.

You might even go into the second stage and decide to avail yourself of some organized benevolence by relating these boys and girls to a local troop of Boy Scouts or Girl Scouts or the nearby Y. But is it not true that if you really cared about the plight of those people this would not be enough for you? You would also become concerned about sanitation standards, building codes, the minimum wage, education for migrant children, etc. Your sincerity would get you talking with other people about these matters. Eventually you would be making your way to Albany or Sacramento or Lansing, and Washington, D.C.! If we wish to do more than put verbal band-aids over people's wounds, we will of necessity involve ourselves in the changing of laws and structures from what they are to what they ought to be.

There is room for imagination and inventiveness at the local level as congregations look for meaningful ways of relating to their neighbors in need. In many instances, perhaps most, the church will find itself anxious to cooperate with some group or movement already on the scene. Some loss of identity is incurred in this tactic of reinforcement, but this is small enough price to pay for our having forfeited the initiative. Besides, who knows the name of the Good Samaritan, anyway?

There will be those other instances, however, when the strategy will be one of initiation rather than cooperation. That is, the local congregation will attempt to start a form of witness or ministry that is path-breaking and new in that place. The minister who attempts to shepherd some innovative program to the point where it wins board approval and congregational support had better brace for battle. God is not limited to forms of service we are accustomed to; but most Christians do not know this. The feeling persists in many congregations that to depart from the familiar is tantamount to departing from God. When a church officer responds to a challenge to start something new by saying, "But we never did that before," it is important that his observation be heard for what it is: a statement of history, and not an argument against.

A church within my knowledge made a careful study of its community and concluded that temporary emergency housing was a critical need that the church could do something about. In due time a proposal was made that the church invest in property for the purpose of meeting this need and engage a social worker, part time, to help the families the church would be serving in this way. Before the proposition carried it had to weather considerable opposition. A prime move to resist this venture came in the form of a statement delivered with the intended force of an axiom to the effect that "the church doesn't belong in the housing business." Had we all the vital records on hand they would doubtless show that when Christian money first went into hospitals, warning voices piously declared that the church had no right to get involved in the healing business. Similar caution doubtless attended the announcement of the first Christian orphanage, the first Christian settlement house, the first Christian literacy campaign, the first Christian coffee house, the first Christian college. These voices should be expected, and they should be courteously heard, but they should not deter us from exercising the boldness and imagination God has given us for the sake of Christ and the gospel.

CHAPTER X

Coping with Ferment

It is hard to read the papers these days without flinching. The FASTEN SEAT BELT sign has been on for a long while, and there is no hint that we will be able to fly over, under, or around the turbulence any time soon. No segment of society has been left unshaken—business, government, education, the home, the church.

When human beings attempt to comprehend the problems that assail them, they frequently put their minds to work in quest of a constant, some factor present in all or many of their troubles, that will help them understand and provide a handle. At the risk of oversimplifying the fix in which we stew, I suggest that what Rhody McCoy said of the 1968 public school crisis in New York City sheds light on a considerable number of our problems. The embattled educator said, "The confrontation is basically one between systems and people."

The system has cowed us and we resent it. The little man today sees himself as a youthful David going out, minus sling or stones, to do battle with Goliath. For this reason primarily, the word institutional has a bad ring to it. It has become a "snarl word" in our vocabulary, especially among the young. The under-thirty generation prefers to experience life directly without benefit of institutional mediation. If I hear them at all it would seem that they want love but not marriage, religious experience but not church, learning but not schools, citizenship but not government. In a thousand different ways institutions of every sort in our society are being put on the spot with the same question that was angrily hurled at Jesus in the Temple by the chief priests, scribes, and elders, "By what authority are you doing these things, or who gave you this authority to do them?" (Mark 11:28).

Assaulted by such pressure, some institutions dig in and determine more than ever to keep things as they are until they have a better shot at returning them to the way they used to be. Those who man such institutions or look for refuge in them are possessed by what one might call the Ponce de Leon anxiety. The Spanish explorer as he sought the Fountain of Youth was nagged and driven by a feeling he could not shake that something vital had slipped away. The Carib Indians of the Lesser Antilles told of an island called Bimini where gold abounded, and delicious fruit, and a spring whose waters had the power to make the aged young again. This became Juan Ponce de Leon's master obsession. Symbolically he represents those who are committed to the belief that something has been lost that needs finding again, that the way ahead lies in the way back, that to be saved is to return. At bottom, the Ponce de Leon anxiety combs out to a refusal to accept the present.

This anxiety takes its toll in virtually every area of our life, but in no institution with greater devastation than the Christian church. Perhaps ministers bear major responsibility here. Which of us has not repeatedly badgered his congregation with generalized references to the early church designed to make present levels of commitment appear woefully inadequate by comparison. Why, to hear us tell it, all who comprised the membership of the church in those years of pure beginnings prayed fervently, gave sacrificially, witnessed bravely, and loved fully! One would think we had never heard of Paul's tiff with Peter or the shameful irregularities of the infant flock at Corinth.

Roman Catholic friends are prone to idealize the medieval church and yearn for a return to conditions that prevailed in the twelfth and thirteenth centuries. American Protestants are partial to the church as it used to be here in these United States a hundred years ago. There is a Ponce de Leon-like nostalgia for "the church in the valley by the wildwood," the church of the Currier and Ives prints, the church that flung clean lines against a rural sky. Those were the days—when the church was the center of all life round about, when thorny and divisive issues like race and poverty were not allowed to intrude, when the spirit of man was touched by the evangelist's hand in revivals that came each year with spring. Mention is seldom made of the fact that the church of those remembered years lived side by side with some of the grossest social and economic evils that ever beset a nation, and said precious little about them!

Other institutions and the people who direct them tend to respond to contemporary pressures by absolutizing change. They operate on the philosophy that anything new is better than anything old. Giddy with illusions of inevitable progress, they major with fanatical dedication in the verb "to adjust." Just what it is that we are adjusting *to* is a question seldom posed. It is enough that one keep his hands on tiller and mainsheet and trim the sails to every gust that blows.

Such neolatry (the worship of the new) is short on the ability to distinguish between a fad and a trend. In one of his books Vance Packard tells of a development in American marketing a few years ago that saw manufacturers of refrigerators celebrate in a big way the advent of colored home units. No longer would a family have to suffer the lifeless surface of an all-white box. Colors to match America's kitchen interiors were now available. Those who had a passion for leading out on such propositions quickly went over to colored refrigerators. Alas for them—in a few short years the move to color proved a failure and the new move was back to white again. Such are the hazards of neolatry. Before giving up an old idea we should be sure to have a better one with which to replace it.

Stewart Udall was speaking sense when he said, "The bright upland of a better world will not come into view until we bring population and human planning into balance. I would have no fear for my country's tomorrows if we would turn toward creative parenthood and creative education, if we already had established the secure foundations of an equal-opportunity society and mastered the sensitive arts of building a life-encouraging environment. At this moment in history," he concluded "we need to realize that:

> Bigger is not better;
> Slower may be faster;
> Less may well mean more."[1]

Surely there must be a better way to cope with ferment than either of these extreme alternatives. In the game of golf it is established protocol that when all the players finally reach the green, the one farthest from the hole putts first. The others, if they are on their toes, will "go to school" on that first putt. They will study it for clues as to whether the green is fast or slow, whether the slant is more pronounced than it looks, whether there are hidden convolutions, etc. Sensitive leaders in America have been going to school on each other's putts over these past ten years or so, as one institution after another has reacted to the crunch of change. The problems that beset the church in such tumultuous times are different in focus but not in substance from the issues that confront our major universities, our trade unions, our public schools, our courts, our legislative bodies. At this writing four lessons emerge and commend themselves to me as wise and workable.

1. We must be flexible. Bridges are built to sway, tall buildings to give a little with the wind, and mighty trees to bend. No church, institutionally speaking, will prove a match for the day armed only with Roberts' *Rules Of Order,* a copy of the bylaws, and the minutes of the last meeting. A fine church in this country located near a major campus received an overture from a small student/faculty group requesting permission to use a nearby building that the church owned, for the purpose of setting up a free university. Admittedly, the free-university movement is considerably left of center in political and social outlook, and the general public is not lining up for the privilege of providing local units with space. Subjects would be taught here that the university was not offering—courses in Red Chinese History, Contemporary Beatnik Poetry, Black History, etc.

The official board of the church sat to work out its response to the request. One member asked whether the group wishing to launch this experiment in education was properly registered on campus. Another wished to know if the group had officers and who they were. Still another inquired about the fiscal responsibility of the group, wondering aloud whether it had a bank account and whether the treasurer was properly bonded. Here was a church accustomed to doing business decently and in order, with a rich history that spanned more than a hundred years, asking a visionary upstart group to qualify as tenant by producing credentials that only venerable organizations could possibly come up with. I am not arguing here for the free university. Rather I am suggesting that flexibility was lacking in that first line of questioning. The church at times is like an electric wall outlet built to take a two-pronged plug. If a three- or four-pronged plug shows up, we are powerless to

receive it. It is a serious matter to withhold dialogue or sponsor-
ship. It could just happen that we turned away an angel
unawares. In a revolutionary day, pedigree is not the paramount
consideration.

Institutions tend to become more conservative in outlook
than they realize. Churches have a way of hearing what they
want to hear by exercising control of the agenda. Recent con-
frontations by Black Militants have at least rocked us from the
smug assurance that the input question is entirely in our hands.
The plea then is for flexibility. Walter Kerr in his delightful
book on *tragedy and comedy* shares these lines:

> In flood time you can see how some trees bend
> And because they bend, even their twigs are safe,
> While stubborn trees are torn up, roots and all.[2]

2. We must increasingly personalize our relationships with
those we serve. In higher education, students resent more and
more the dehumanizing effects of a system that partakes of the
weaknesses of mass production. Senior professors are seldom
seen at the undergraduate level. They are even scarce at the
graduate level, since those who are out to establish a reputation
move away from teaching in the interest of more prestigious
writing and research. One distraught student, fortunate enough
to have been admitted to a course that found him sharing
thrice-weekly lectures with three hundred other students, com-
plained that the learned professor at each session "popped in,
popped off, and popped out."

Are things much better in the church? Do people sense that
they matter to God because they matter to us? Do we take
seriously their views and impressions of the church? Have we
worked out ways to involve them in the decision-making
process before the decision happens? These questions must be

raised, because even within the church we have a way of using people for programmatic ends.

University presidents who have demonstrated an ability to cope effectively with ferment—men like Robben Fleming of the University of Michigan; Ferrel Heady of the University of New Mexico; Roger Heynes, Chancellor at Berkeley; and Andrew Cordier of Columbia, to name a few—are without exception men who are approachable and open. Rigidity is not an asset in a time when landmarks fall.

Dr. Eugene Jennings has observed that

there is one type of boss who drives away almost every young man or woman who comes his way. Unfortunately, he happens to be like the majority of my generation. He was taught to obey first and think second. If you diagram his character, you find that he operates more by rules of thumb and principles than by perception, learning and facts.

The younger generation is just the opposite. They are the why-whys. They distrust rules and suspect that men who shout rules are incompetent. They go for facts, for analysis of the problem. They were raised to think first and obey second.[3]

There are basically but two kinds of authority in the world: authority that is *extrinsic* to the holder and almost wholly dependent on rank and title, and authority that is *intrinsic* to the holder, emanating from what he is as a person and only indirectly related to the position he fills. Extrinsic leadership is a falling star in today's sky. The leadership in demand now is leadership that wants to listen and knows how to do so.

The frail oboe has intrigued me ever since that day in high school when a member of the music department almost talked me into taking it up. Lovers of symphonic music are well aware that orchestras tune to the oboe. For years I thought this was because the oboe was mysteriously possessed of perfect pitch.

Loud was the fall of that unfounded notion when I learned
that orchestras tune to the oboe because the oboe cannot be
tuned. The other instruments must adjust or brace for chaos.

There are ministers in the Christian churches of the land
who have insisted that congregations docilely tune up (or
down) to their views of worship, their theology, their understanding of mission, their slant on current social, economic, and
political matters—or else! That style of leadership is having a
tough time of it now. People insist on being taken seriously.
They are not entitled to prevail, but they do deserve to be heard.
The man whose leadership is conferred instead of earned belongs to a vanishing breed. It might be said of him, what Angus
said of Macbeth:

> Those he commands moves only in command,
> Nothing in love: now does he feel his title
> Hang loose about him, like a giant's robe
> Upon a dwarfish thief.[4]

3. I would suggest as a further lesson worth learning that
every institution in our society must work in interdependence
with other institutions in order to fulfill its role. Business
corporations must be constructively related to the needs of the
encircling community, universities must be attentive to their
immediate social and physical environment, churches must make
their witness in the public sector in concert with viable political,
educational, medical, and business institutions.

Churches that yearn to be relevant in our metropolitan centers
will not be long at the job before they discover that many of
the problems they face on behalf of the city's beleaguered in-
habitants have regional dimensions and will yield only to regional solutions. Margaret Mead makes this point with telling
effectiveness as she speaks to the problem of water pollution:

"It is argued that Lake Erie is dead not only because there was no agency equipped to think ecologically about what was happening to its waters, but that, in fact, Lake Erie and its environs is too small a system to have dealt with if, in fact, there had been any group or agency charged with preventing the Lake Erie disaster. It is further argued that if, instead, the whole Great Lake region is considered together, then it might be possible to make the kind of predictions which could be tested in advance."[5]

4. I would offer as a fourth lesson the conviction that institutions must learn to draw the line between what is negotiable and what is not. Unchecked permissiveness is not a virtue. Child psychologists whom I have read are united in the belief that parents who yield to their children on everything are rendering their offspring a damaging disservice. It belongs to the nature of children to discover how far they can go. At the same time, they want to know where the bounds of their freedom lie. Parents who fail to draw the line that says "thus far and no further" hurt their children by imagined kindness.

One of America's distinguished university presidents bravely made his way to a student rally that had been engineered by a group of disgruntled dissidents. Already he had established a reputation for fairness and approachability. In the question period that capped the evening off an irate student rose to his feet to declare that he was tired of being told what subjects he had to take. He wanted the academic freedom to scan the university catalogue and select whatever subjects appealed to him. The president, responding in a firm but friendly voice, said: "Students at this university have always been allowed to take whatever subjects they wish. This privilege is open to you. But you cannot take just any subjects you wish and receive a Bachelor of Arts degree!" The prexy had drawn the line. At the point where an academic degree was about to be debased for past and present student generations, the very essence of the university was threatened and a stand had to be made.

Liberal spirits in the church must be prepared to draw the line where the essence of the church is threatened. I have been amazed over the past two decades at the number of groups and individuals who have renounced and buried the church but who nonetheless have sought to tune our pulpits or use the church's assets for their purposes. The urge to accommodate is Christian, but there is a point beyond which we cannot go if we are to retain our identity as the redeemed of Christ. My colleague in the ministry William Gray, pastor of the Downtown Presbyterian Church in Nashville, Tennessee, put the matter this way.

How far out do you go before you become something else? How low can you turn the light before it becomes part of the darkness? At what point does being become non-being, and where does matter become anti-matter?

How far into the secular can the sacred be taken before it becomes secular itself? How far can a person go in indulging his prejudices before he must confess that he is unregenerate? How far back can a person backslide before he has parted company, perhaps eternally, with the community of God?[6]

We stand in the zone where tragedy is born, the contested terrain where the insolent new is locked in deadly combat with the yielding but still resisting old. We did not volunteer for the assignment, but here we are, in the kingdom for such a time as this. God make us equal to the task!

CHAPTER XI

Continuity and Change

In January of 1928 William Allen White received a letter from Secretary of State Elihu Root in which the Cabinet member said, "I like your stirring up of the crust formed by conventions because at the same time you do not abjure the accumulated wisdom of the race, which institutions are formed to preserve and which the same institutions, if they are left alone, will always tend to smother. Just where the line comes between preserving and smothering it seems difficult to determine, and there are constantly honest differences of opinion which nobody has any right to get mad about! That is the essence of liberty."[1] Root put his finger on one of history's most persistent and vexing tensions—the tension between continuity and change. The church by its very nature is a conserver of all that is good in the past. At the same time it is committed to history's ever-leading, always-moving Lord. This paradox visits individual Christians with painful force at those points in their pilgrimage where they are forced to decide for or against change.

To change or not to change. It is a matter of urgent importance that we ask whether there is such a thing as a Christian response to change. Must our attitude toward change be determined by our political affiliations, our economic status, the friends we keep, the number of birthdays we have celebrated, the temperament with which God has endowed us? Or should our faith in God give us a mind-set that will make us either resist or welcome change?

It is perplexing to note that throughout the course of Christian history, some believers have felt that they were doing what God wanted when they resisted change, while others were convinced that they were serving God when they fostered change. The most helpful statement on this dilemma that I have come upon is by Max L. Stackhouse of Andover Newton Theological School. He observes, "At stake in this dispute, we might suggest, are complex issues. One is a primal perception as to whether the 'problem' with history is that it continually threatens to break into chaos and must be ever and again ordered constructively toward righteousness, or whether the 'problem' of history is that it has been over-institutionalized and ordered so that new freedoms and creativities cannot break forth. In short, is the creative continuity of history to be found in breaking free from false bondage or providing frames for organized purpose?"[2]

The man of conservative temperament believes that chaos is always trying to break in upon us to destroy, and that God's man will be found resolutely on the side of order. The liberal spirit, perhaps tinged a bit by Rousseau, believes that the institutionalization of life is what impedes the human spirit. In God's name, therefore, he goes out to minimize or overthrow the power of the institutional. We must allow that both positions can be held with equally sincere motivation. But this doesn't help us know whether to resist or encourage change.

The very Scriptures themselves are ambiguous at this point. In Ecclesiastes we read, "For everything there is a season, and a time for every matter under heaven." What does this say? The writer of those well-known words goes on to indicate the various kinds of time: "a time to plant and a time to pluck up what is planted; . . . a time to break down and a time to build up; . . . a time to rend and a time to sew" (Eccles. 3:1, 2*b*, 3*b*, 7*a*). But what time is it now? His words are beautifully descriptive but fall short of being helpful.

Israel's mission in the main was a mission of conservation. Israel had to conserve monotheism against the threat of polytheism, the worship of God in spirit against the threat of idolatry, the covenant community against the threat of assimilation, so that out of Israel's loins Messiah might come. There were times in Israel's history when the liberal voice had to be resisted. As for example on those occasions when there was counsel in the direction of an alliance with Egypt or Assyria. Such a change in national policy would have been wrong and contrary to the will of God. And there were those other times when not to change would have been to violate God's will. As, for example, when God was moving His people from a nomadic kind of life to an urban life; when He was moving them from a theocracy to a monarchy; when, in the postexilic period, He was moving them from an ultra-exclusivism to a more inclusive society as embodied in the story of Ruth.

Is it then a matter of a coin toss? Is it a matter of my reacting to change as a Republican or a Democrat? As a black man or a white man? As a poor or a rich man? As a sophisticate or a philistine? As a daring individual or a timid? Let me suggest that while a baffling ambiguity must prevail, there are at least four facts that Christians should reckon with in deciding what their stance should be toward change.

First is the recognition that growth belongs to life, and that without change there can be no growth. Maturity, progress, development—all of these are impossible without change. Pierre Teilhard de Chardin has been celebrated far and wide because he has made the church, among other institutions, aware that

God's creation is not yet finished. In his writings he gave us an exciting, eruptive and expansive kind of universe. Years ago John Henry Newman did the same thing for the world of ideas. In a rather remarkable essay entitled, "On the Process of Development in Ideas," Newman grappled with the question whether truth in its origin is not to be preferred to truth in its subsequent development. He writes,

It is sometimes said that the stream is clearest near the spring. Whatever use may fairly be made of this image, it does not apply to the history of a philosophy or belief, which on the contrary is more equable and purer, and stronger, when its bed has become deep, and broad, and full. It necessarily rises out of an existing state of things, and for a time savors of the soil. Its vital element needs disengaging from what is foreign and temporary, and is employed in efforts after freedom which become more vigorous and hopeful as its years increase.

In time it enters upon strange territory; points of controversy alter their bearing; parties rise and fall around it; danger and hopes appear in new relations; and old principles reappear under new forms. It changes with them in order to remain the same. In a higher world it is otherwise, but here below to live is to change, and to be perfect is to have changed often.[3]

To oppose change is, in most instances, to obstruct growth.

A second factor that must be reckoned with as we seek to develop a Christian stance toward change is the simple awareness that, being human, we tend to cling tenaciously to what is customary and familiar. We men begin to shave from the same side of the face each morning. We never change. Most of us have our own peculiar way of reading a newspaper, and we never change. Most of us put on either the left shoe or the right shoe first every time we dress. When we are faced with change, the sin of sloth becomes a very strong temptation. We are just plain too lazy to make an adjustment to the new. How easily we become addicted to the familiar, forgetting that we are called to be pilgrims, and that the patron saint of faith is Abraham, who went out not knowing whither he went.

A third fact to be considered is that, our pride being what it is, we tend to want what is good for us and resist what is bad for us. That is to say, we tend, unless we make a contrary effort, to make our decisions on the basis of self-reference. We must learn to discount in ourselves and in others arguments that rise from self-interest. We must discount the argument of the theater owner against pay TV. We must discount the argument of the gun manufacturer against a gun-control law. We must discount the argument of the millionaire against the graduated income tax or a stiffer inheritance tax. We must discount the argument of the relief recipient who wants his monthly income quadrupled. In all of these self-interest obviously plays too strong a role.

I asked a friend one day, "How do you know whether you should be for change or not?" His answer was simple and direct, "If it hurts, it's good." If something I opt for will hurt me in the wallet, if it will get me out of familiar patterns and customs, if there is pain of adjustment, chances are, as a rule of thumb, it's good.

There are some very lovely homes up along the Delaware River that will presently be destroyed in the interest of the Tock Island Project. A new dam and national park is in the planning stages. There were protests, naturally, from those who have enjoyed their riverfront cottages for years. At last, however, this counsel prevailed: the few would have to sacrifice their personal enjoyment for the good of the greater number.

The fourth fact to be brought into view as we contemplate a stance toward change is this: the church, unless it takes pains to be otherwise, will be an obstacle to change. The church by nature is cautious and conservative. It likes to wear a belt and suspenders. Perhaps the Freudian slip that betrays the church's attitude toward change is to be found in a line of one of Christendom's most beloved hymns, "Abide with Me." In the second stanza, Henry F. Lyte wrote: "Change and decay in all around I see; O thou who changest not, abide with me."[4] What an unfortunate and unwarranted linkage, that *change* should be equated with *decay!* I come more and more to believe that this is the church's basic stance toward change, unless it is diligent to overcome it.

The church comes by this position understandably. After all, a large part of the church's mission is to stand for continuity in society. Church is a place where the ages speak to the moments. We are here to keep ourselves and the world in remembrance of a love that will not let us go. We do this by reiteration, by ritual, by the celebration of the sacraments, by preaching, by singing, by praying. Because this ministry of continuity is so much a part of what we are trying to do, a sameness overtakes our ecclesiastical life, so that our organizations look today just about the way they looked twenty years ago. Our official meetings go on and on, more or less centering on matters that have to do with ecclesiastical housekeeping. *The new doesn't have a chance to get in unless it is brought in deliberately with conviction and persuasion.*

The second reason why this is true is because, quite frankly, the church has developed a dependence on the system. We have buildings to maintain, programs to finance, staffs to employ. It is logical to expect that income for the church will come from those who are satisfied with the system as it is. You can't expect much support from the have-nots, so you learn to look for it from the haves, and the haves like the way things are because the system has been good to them. *The church has learned through the years to lower its voice in order to raise its budget.*

Finally, the church tends to "sit it out" because no absolutes stand out to capture her imagination and command her energies. The result is a church that tends to drift further and further away from reality. And let it be remembered that the irrelevant church is the foremost barrier to evangelism. There is a Christian camp on the West Coast with a sign at its entranceway that says, "One mile closer to heaven." A youngster from that camp went to the Deep South for a few weeks to work with the black minority. When she came back, she changed that sign and made it read, "One mile further from earth."

Isaac Newton gave as one of the laws of motion that "bodies at rest tend to remain at rest." Even ecclesiastical bodies at rest, tend to remain at rest! Every church needs to give prime visibility to a council or committee expressly charged with the responsibility of making the congregation face up to issues in the political, social, and economic sectors that by nature it would prefer to avoid. Such a body will create awareness within the membership and suggest action programs through which the church's witness can be made.

To change or not to change, this is the question. But to change or not to change as those who call Christ Lord—this is the context in which the answer must be sought.

CHAPTER XII

The Case for Reparations

On Sunday morning, May 4, 1969, Mr. James Foreman, representing the National Black Economic Development Conference, issued a "Black Manifesto" to the Christian churches of the land in general and the Riverside Church in particular. The key issue in the document, as is well known now, is the issue of reparations. Mr. Foreman's confrontation touched off a volley of journalistic comment, letters to the editor, sermons, and gut discussions at the sidewalk level. Those whose racism throbs just beneath the surface used the document and the circumstances attending its publication to put the black man down again. Much of the mail we received in the weeks following Mr. Foreman's visit reflected an inability to admit that corporate guilt is a valid Christian category, and an unwillingness to concede that white Christians in this country owe the black man anything.

I confess that from the start I was sympathetic to the reparations concept. The revolutionary language of the Manifesto troubles me even now, but the charge that white Christians have conspired by their silence in the exploitation of the black man in this country seems to my mind and conscience irrefutable. The following is a sermon delivered at the Riverside Church some ten weeks following the day of confrontation. I place it here toward the end of the book in the hope that what has gone before will help explain convictions argued here.

The Sermon*

There are safer and more manageable subjects for a lazy Sunday in midsummer than the one we have singled out today: "The Case For Reparations." But there is a tide in the affairs of men that is no respecter of preferences. Some themes choose us, we do not choose them.

One thing I need not do today is win you to an affection for Zacchaeus. You already like this friend of Jesus. Most everyone does. Handicapped by a lack of height, he draws us out. With a name like Zacchaeus he probably sat in the back row in school and missed a lot of what went on up front. But chiefly we warm to Zacchaeus because in his zeal to see the Man from Nazareth he was willing to abandon his dignity by running down the street and climbing a tree.

Jesus rewarded Zacchaeus' zeal by stopping before that tree and bidding the publican come down. "Zacchaeus," said Jesus, "Make haste and come down; for I must stay at your house today" (Luke 19:5).

It must have been a walk to end all walks, that walk of Jesus and Zacchaeus to the publican's house. If only we could have bugged *that* conversation. Zacchaeus was a tax collector. His job was to raise money from his own people on behalf of the occupying country, hated Rome. As I understand it, it was a cost-plus operation. He paid so much for the franchise and all that he made beyond that price was his. It was a case of "all the traffic can bear." Apparently Zacchaeus saw to it that the traffic bore plenty.

But now it's different! Zacchaeus sees his job in a new light. He sees other people as he had not seen them before. He sees money in what for him is a startlingly fresh perspective. Listen

*"The Case for Reparations" appeared in *Theology Today* (October 1969) and is reprinted with the permission of *Theology Today*.

to him now! "Behold, Lord, the half of my goods I give to the poor; and if I have defrauded any one of anything I restore it fourfold" (Luke 19:8). Walking with Jesus will do that to a man.

More important than this remarkable resolution of Zacchaeus is the response of Jesus. He pronounces words of unqualified approval. He gives it his blessing. He speaks the reassuring "Amen." For Jesus said to him, "Today salvation has come to this house, since he also is a son of Abraham" (Luke 19:9).

There were two elements in the reclamation of Zacchaeus: *Generosity,* "Half of my goods I give to the poor," and *Justice,* "If I have defrauded any one of anything I restore it fourfold." To put it differently, Zacchaeus made reparation. Let's not fear the term. The principle is as old as the Book of Exodus, and as new as contemporary jurisprudence. In the twenty-second chapter of Exodus we read, "If a man steals an ox or a sheep, and kills it or sells it, he shall pay five oxen for an ox, and four sheep for a sheep. He shall make restitution. . . ." Roman law insisted that a man who stole had to repay fourfold. Zacchaeus goes beyond Roman law by suggesting that he will make amends for any injustice he may have been responsible for.

The principle has a place in Jewish theology. I quote from the *Standard Jewish Encyclopedia*: "Forgiveness of sin depends upon true repentance while a wrong done to a fellowman requires rectification and restitution before forgiveness is possible."[1] Roman Catholic moral theology puts it this way. "Restitution is an act of commutative justice whereby property is restored to one who has been deprived of it by unjust damage or threat."[2]

It wasn't so long ago that a very reputable, conservative, orthodox Baptist theologian, A. H. Strong, writing on repentance, said: "True repentance is indeed manifested and evidenced by confession of sin before God and by *reparation* for wrongs done to men."[3] It was out of such consideration that the World Council of Churches in its first consultation ever on racism, held in London in May 1969, endorsed the principle of reparation. Forgiveness without reparation becomes an indulgence in cheap grace. "Behold, Lord . . . if I have defrauded any one of anything, I restore it fourfold" (Luke 19:8).

It is against this background that our response to the Black Manifesto should be made. Surely it is beyond dispute by now that the white man in this country has not done right by the black man. Before a black child says his first word or takes his first step in our society he is handicapped. The discrimination we work is *sometimes personal* and *always systemic*. That system dates back to slavery, which was instituted by our fathers, but it has been perpetuated and confirmed by us, their sons, to our political, material, and social advantage.

Wherein have we sinned, you ask?

We have sinned as educators by failing to give Americans, black and white, a knowledge of the history of this country's largest minority group.

We have sinned as jurists by finding one loophole after another with which to strangle the black man's hope for justice.

We have sinned as parents by passing on to our children the myth of white supremacy and enforcing it by innuendo, poor example, and sick humor.

We have sinned as tourists by coming up against "white only" signs in restaurants, hotels, swimming pools, and theaters without so much as a word of protest.

We have sinned as sports fans by cheering the exploits of the black athlete and caring little for his welfare as a person.

We have sinned as bankers by restricting the flow of capital into the black community.

We have sinned as trade unionists by denying apprentice status to blacks and failing to welcome them as fellow workers.

We have sinned as members of clubs, fraternities, and lodges by restricting membership to people like ourselves.

We have sinned as legislators by catering to racist pressures and encumbering the path to justice with laws designed to retard progress and make elementary right and wrong appear more complicated than they need to be.

We have sinned as members of the entertainment world by foisting on the American public an image of the black man as a shiftless, drawling, less than human thing.

And we have sinned as ministers of the gospel by stooping to deliver bland assurances that all was well, while the acids of racism were eating away the nation's soul and driving Jesus back to Golgotha!

Our greatest failure as a church lies in our unwillingness or inability, or both, to carry faith beyond the interpersonal level and make it operative at the social and corporate levels.

Martin Luther gave us a good steer when he said, "One who lives in a community must do his share in bearing and suffering the community's burdens, dangers, and injuries, even though, not he, but his neighbor has caused them: He must do this in the same way that he enjoys the peace, profit, protection, wealth, freedom and convenience of the community, even though he has not won them or brought them into being."[4]

We have had the numbers and the power to make a difference, and we have not made that difference. Therein lies our guilt. They also sin who only stand and watch!

We have failed collectively as white Christians, and we can make amends collectively. This is what reparation means to me. Oh, I know there are objections! I've been combing them out of my hair for the last two months. How can damage to a man's soul be repaid by money? It can't. What we have done to the black man in this country is beyond repayment in terms of dollars and cents. We untribed him, we unfamilied him, we unmanned him.

I confess that I could not read without weeping that section in the *Autobiography of Malcolm X*, where he talks about going to Chicago to get a new name to replace the one we had given him when his family was a chattel in the slave system. Listen to him: "My application had, of course, been made and during this time I received from Chicago my X. The Muslim's X symbolized the true African family name that he never could know. For me, my "X" replaced the white slave-master name of "Little" which some blue-eyed devil name Little had imposed upon my paternal forebear. The receipt of my "X" means that forever after in the nation of Islam, I would be known as Malcolm X. Mr. Muhammad taught that we would keep this "X" until God Himself returned and gave us a Holy Name from His own mouth."[5] There is no money that can make up for this. But our money can be an earnest of a good intention and hint at a new direction for the Church and for the nation.

"Why can't we call it something other than reparations? I don't like the term." More is involved than a squabble over semantics. The term must be reckoned with not only because it is in the Manifesto but because once we get away from it we are going to do again what "Whitey" has done for hundreds of years, make a few gifts here and there and pride ourselves on our generosity. All such gifts have a way of flattering the donor and debasing the recipient. *That which we are called upon to do does not come under the category of generosity. It belongs to justice.* The term reparation insures that insight. The Good Samaritan was generous. He only *found* his victim in the ditch, we *put* ours there.

"But others have claims—the American Indian, the Spanish American, the Eskimo, the deprived people of Appalachia.

Where does the whole thing end?" One claim does not cancel out another. What sort of logic is this? *Each case* deserves its day in court before the conscience of the church and nation.

"Isn't it morbid to talk about guilt? Isn't it depressing? Doesn't it have a backward look and make impossible that forward-looking stance so sorely needed?"

Most people who feel this way have a habit of coupling the word "guilt" with prejudicial qualifiers. They talk about "morbid" guilt or "fruitless" introspection. As any minister or priest knows full well, guilt *can become* pathological. One can become excessively preoccupied with it. But this need not be so. I am not suggesting that guilt should be the only component of our response to the black people. I insist that it is a component. True repentance has a way of not only looking back, but of motivating us for the work that waits our doing.

"What difference would it make if this church and every other church got with it?" Not much. There isn't all that much wealth even with old and new money combined. But the church could very well be used of God as a catalytic agent to loosen sizable sums from others sectors of American life, notably business and government.

"Why should we help the black man? My parents were foreign born. They came over and made good without any outside help" The answer is that the cases are not similar. Your parents came voluntarily. These people were brought over under our compulsion. Moreover, by the accident of color they were denied assimilation into normal American life—a deprivation European immigrants did not face.

The most serious objection of all, however, is this. "Why should I support a revolution?" My answer is "You shouldn't. And you don't have to!" One of the most distinguished theologians in American Protestantism confided to me privately how regretful he was that we do not have a better document as a symbol of the current confrontation. He was referring to the fact that the Black Manifesto has a sad way of confusing two issues —reparations and revolution. Revolution is always a possibility. We went that route ourselves vis-à-vis England. Doubtless there will always be some in any political state who are convinced that revolution is called for. They will act accordingly. *But it is madness to expect people who do not share that conviction to contribute to it.* Suicide no less than racism is a sin.

Tragically the Black Manifesto puts two loyalties on a collision course—a belated loyalty to the black man in his quest for justice, and a loyalty to country. It is a recognized parliamentary procedure that a member who requests it may have a question divided. I ask, therefore, that this question be divided. Reparations? Yes! Revolution? No! As clearly as I can I want to say that no funds that I give, no funds that I raise, no funds over which I have an influence will be used for the destruction or overthrow of this government. I believe we need reform. I believe we stand in need of drastic overhaul and renewal from the inside out. But I don't believe God is finished yet with this republic!

If the revolutionary talk in the Manifesto, the Marxist line that marks its opening pages, was only an attention-getting device, it has served its purpose and ought to be honorably retired, so that we can get on with the business of making reparations that lead, not to revolution, but to reconciliation. "God was in Christ reconciling the world to himself . . . *and hath committed unto us the word of reconciliation"* (II Cor. 5:19—italics mine). This is our ultimate commitment as Christians.

Let me change the figure and introduce at the same time a touching bit of dialogue from John Steinbeck's play, *The Short Reign of Pippin IV.* The king in disguise comes to the little French town of Gambais, where he notices as he nears a castle that a bust of Pan has been removed from its pedestal and thrown into the moat. Pippin asks an old man, "How did it get in the moat?" "Oh, someone pushed him in. They always do, sometimes two or three times a year." "But why?" "Who knows?" said the old man. "There's people that push things in the moat. Pretty hard work too. There's just people that push things in the moat."

A little later the king asks gently, "Are you the owner here?" "No," he said, "I'm not. I live hereabouts." "Then why do you pull them out?" The old man looked puzzled and searched for an answer. "Why—I don't know. I guess there's people that pull things out—that's what they do. I guess that's how things get done."[6] People who push things in and people who pull things out—we have a choice.

Rather than begrudge reparations I should think that we would rejoice that our sin in part is reparationable. How that drunk hit-and-run driver who killed a little girl last night wishes he could make reparation! We still have time, and history has remained sufficiently set, to allow us this response.

I am not presumptuous enough to suggest that this is *the Christian* response to reparation. I am simply saying that it is *this Christian's response.* "And Zacchaeus stood and said to the Lord, 'If I have defrauded any one of anything, I restore it fourfold" (Luke 19:8). What do *you* make of *that!*

CHAPTER XIII

The Vital Balance

As churches in this country come to maturity and begin to take seriously the claims of justice as well as the Great Commission (Matt. 28:18), there is always the possibility that the pendulum will swing too far the other way. It frequently happens thus with ministers who can no longer abide the church's lack of engagement with the world, and who move with deliberate, and often not so deliberate, speed to remedy the situation.

Such is the way with human nature, redeemed or not: that we tend to overcorrect when we get down to the business of making things right. There are clergymen and laymen in these United States in considerable numbers who have surrendered their Christian birthright for a whopping bowlful of the porridge of relevance. Bent on changing systems, they lose both the desire and the ability to be used of God in changing men. Enamored of the behavioral sciences, they neglect the weightier analysis of human nature contained in the Scriptures. Impressed by psychiatry's insistence that man's surface problems are of unconscious, subconscious, and complicated origin, they lose confidence in the power of the love of God to take a man where he is and make him a new creation. Their imagination captured by the world's way of marshaling and applying power, they are embarrassed to be identified with the weapons of the Spirit, which on the promise of the Scriptures are mighty to the pulling down of strongholds (II Cor. 10:4).

The quest for relevance becomes a cruel master. It plays tricks on a man's perspective and tends to orient him more toward quick and measurable results than to fidelity of witness. An odd twist to the passion for relevance lies in the observation that most of us have a habit of thinking that the other fellow has more of it than we do. This is another version of the "greener grass" obsession that keeps us hankering for the other hill. Ministers drop out of their pastorates and become social workers to become relevant. At the same time social workers are coming the other way for the same reason.

Politicians think that clergymen have relevance, while clergymen inwardly pine for the relevance and political power of legislators and other elected officials. Teachers think lawyers are where the action is, and barristers frequently wish they were in every way such as the teachers are, except for their salaries. Perhaps one day we will tumble to the truth that relevance resides more in the person than in the position. A loser will be a loser wherever he is placed. No position is the right position in the lineup for a .200 hitter. A man who is fully awake to God and to the world around him will be a catalytic agent and make things happen whatever his chosen field or place of service.

An autobiography that found me in time of need and exercised a shaping influence on the pattern of my ministry was that of D. R. Davies. This author is better known for *Down Peacock Feathers* and *On to Orthodoxy,* but I am in his debt chiefly for the honest writing in his own life story, *In Search of Myself.*[1]

Davies, a Welshman, was born to a personal knowledge of

the poverty, deprivations, and hazards of that country's mining communities. His father was a miner and gave his son a living introduction to a system that cried out for wage and safety reform.

Having felt the call to the ministry, Davies became an ordained clergyman in the Congregational Church. Determined to make the church a potent force for change, he preached on social issues constantly and was an astute enough administrator to be able in time to "load" the governing boards of the church with laymen of like persuasion. He became a valued and prominent member of the Labour Party and turned his church into one of its more influential centers.

In time Davies discovered that the church he served was lacking in inner unity and purpose because many of its members were held together by a commitment, not to Jesus Christ, but to a political ideology that focused on the strife of class with class. He speaks movingly of the church he had fashioned in his ardent but misdirected zeal.

The result was, though I did not realize it at the time, that there were admitted into church membership scores of people who cared less than nothing for the New Testament Gospel, and who were innocent of any fundamental Christian experience. In effect, the church degenerated into a branch of the Labour Party. The services were predominantly political, hymns, prayers, the lesson (frequently read from outside the Bible) and the sermon, especially the sermon. Since the main purpose of Jesus was to create a new social order, I used to say, the true business of the church was to agitate against Capitalism, which was the chief obstacle to the new order. That was the task of the church, if-IF-Christ's mission was to create a new social order on earth, if by Kingdom of God He meant merely a new civilization. What I did was to draw, simply and directly, the essential logical conclusion from that idea. I converted a Christian Church into a political organization—and remained Congregational. I was

sincere of course, but I had betrayed the Gospel. With neither authority nor dogma, as my case proved, the Gospel (and the Church)
are defenseless against the vagaries and moods of the individual.[2]

In due time Davies left the ministry of the Congregational
Church. After an interlude of somber reflection he returned to
the Christian ministry as a priest in the Anglican communion.

Davies' story is a poignant and compelling illustration of
what is happening to many men in the American church today.
We seem to live on the assumption that one must choose between Christ and service in the world. Is it naïve to believe
that one can be both true to Christ and a progressive member
of the world community at the same time?

I cling to the hope that no congregation need make an
either/or choice at this point. At the same time I acknowledge
that the desired balance is elusive and only rarely achieved. A
church that draws its sustenance from a Bible that contains in
one place "The Lord is my shepherd; I shall not want" (Ps.
23:1), and in another "Let justice roll down like waters, and
righteousness like an everflowing stream" (Amos 5:24), should
be able to purpose in its soul to speak to personal religion and
corporate affairs without feeling guilty about either.

However poorly we approximate the goal, it should be our
aim in the ministry so to declare the gospel and administer a
parish that man's inner longing and temporal necessities alike
may be addressed. The personal gospel–social gospel framework was from its inception misleading and divisive. There is
but one gospel, grounded in God's gracious, saving deed in
Jesus Christ and relevant to all the life that we are called upon
to live in this world and the next.

I have asked myself many times in recent years what the
balance for which this volume pleads would look like if it came.
Would a given congregation that had achieved such balance
be made up of individual members who were equally at home

putting together a fair housing ordinance and praying at the bedside of the sick? Perhaps in some rare cases such roundedness might be found. Twenty years in the pastoral ministry, however, lead me to believe that such a hope is unrealistic. Besides, a man who tries to be all things to all men is likely to be nothing much to anyone. The carefully balanced Christian is usually void of the passion that gets things done and makes its mark on the world. He is like the academician who knows all the points of view on a given matter and champions none.

No, the balance is to be looked for not in the individual but in the congregation. Wholeness resides in the body, not in any of its members. A church of any size at all will have in it those who keep alive the will to pray, those who are committed to the teaching of the young, those who are bent on keeping public worship exciting and theologically sound, those who have a zeal to bring others to the side of Christ, those who billboard the church's responsibility to the world at large, and those who are insistently determined to make the gospel relevant to pressing social and political needs.

Kenneth Boulding, speaking of human society, observes that "there are many things that one man can do because other people are not doing them. If everybody at the same time decided to go downtown, draw money out of the bank or even pay their debts, the whole system would collapse."[3] The principle holds true for the church. What mayhem, if all the members of the church showed up to sing in the choir or turned out to work with the young people! Others release me for my specialty by tending to their own. As St. Paul wrote, surely with a smile, "If the whole body were an eye, where would be the hearing? If the whole body were an ear, where would be the sense of smell? But as it is, God arranged the organs in the body, each one of them, as he chose" (I Cor. 12:17-18).

Differences in aptitude and vision make for an awakened and

stimulating church. Unity is preserved through it all because each member has confidence in his own experience of God and respect for the experiences of others. Each special interest group within such a congregation will know in its honest moments that it has been freed to concentrate on one emphasis because others, equally dedicated, are attending to other emphases every bit as vital to the cause.

The unity will flow from a common allegiance, shared by all the members, for Jesus Christ, the head of the body. St. Paul described this unity winsomely when he wrote: "He is the head, and on him the whole body depends. Bonded and knit together by every constituent joint, the whole frame grows through the due activity of each part, and builds itself up in love" (Eph. 4:16, NEB).

Notes

CHAPTER I *The Option We Tend to Forget*

1. *Julius Caesar,* Act II, Scene 1.
2. Presented by Carl McIntire for the International Council of Christian Churches on September 14, 1969, outside The Riverside Church, New York City.
3. Letter to the Editor, *New York Times,* September 7, 1969, from John Mogey, Professor of Sociology at Boston University.
4. Walter Rauschenbusch, *Christianity and the Social Crisis* (New York: The Macmillan Co., 1907), p. 367.

CHAPTER II *Lord of What?*

1. Sören Kierkegaard, *Training in Christianity,* trans. by Walter Lowrie (Princeton: Princeton University Press, 1947).
2. James Stewart, *A Man in Christ* (New York: Harper & Brothers, 1953).
3. Wilfred Cantwell Smith, *The Meaning and End of Religion* (New York: Mentor Books, 1962), p. 116.
4. Kenneth Cauthen, *Science, Secularization and God* (Nashville: Abingdon Press, 1967), p. 211.
5. Mrs. Hamilton King, "The Disciples," quoted in William Temple, *Nature, Man and God* (London: Macmillan & Co., 1953), p. 511.

CHAPTER III *On Taking History Seriously*

1. Arend Th. van Leeuwen, *Christianity in World History,* (London: Edinburgh House Press, 1964), p. 36.

2. December 9, 1961.
3. Emil Brunner, *Justice and the Social Order* (New York: Harper & Brothers, 1945), p. 116.

CHAPTER IV *Two Cheers for Christian Secularity!*

1. William Barrett, *Irrational Man* (Garden City, N.Y.: Doubleday & Co., 1958), p. 102.
2. Carlyle Marney, *The Recovery of the Person* (Nashville: Abingdon Press, 1963), p. 38.
3. Hendrikus Berkhof, *Christ and the Powers,* John Yoder, trans. (Scottdale, Pa.: Herald Press, 1962).
4. D. T. Niles, *Ecumenical Review,* Vol. XX, No. 4 (1968), p. 391.
5. Hendrikus Berkhof, *Christ the Meaning of History* (Richmond, Va.: John Knox Press, 1966), p. 91.
6. *Ibid.,* p. 98.
7. John Bennett, Address to the Class of 1966 at Princeton Seminary, June 7, 1966, printed in the Seminary *Alumni News,* Summer 1966.
8. Nicholas Berdyaev, *Dream and Reality,* Katharine Lampert, trans. (New York: The Macmillan Co., 1951), p. 307.
9. Ursula Solek, "What Shall We Say?" *Presbyterian Life,* June 1, 1967. Reprinted with permission.

CHAPTER V *The Conversion-First Hangup*

1. Will Herberg, *Protestant-Catholic-Jew* (New York: Doubleday—Anchor Books, 1960), p. 116.

CHAPTER VII *The Silence of the New Testament*

1. R. E. C. Browne, *Dictionary of Christian Ethics,* John Macquarrie, ed. (Philadelphia: Westminster Press, 1967), p. 295.

CHAPTER VIII *Christ Our Contemporary*

1. Max Mueller, *Natural Religion* (New York: Longmans, Green & Co., 1889).
2. Karl Barth, *Evangelical Theology,* Grover Foley, trans. (New York: Holt, Rinehart & Winston, 1963), ch. III.
3. William DeWitt Hyde, "Creation's Lord, We Give Thee Thanks," *Pilgrim Hymnal* (Boston: Pilgrim Press, 1958), No. 303.

CHAPTER IX *Getting On with It*

1. Emil Brunner, *op. cit.,* p. 128.
2. *Selected Plays of Sean O'Casey* (New York: George Braziller, 1956), p. 16.
3. From *The Carolina Israelite,* July-August, 1964.

CHAPTER X *Coping with Ferment*

1. Stewart L. Udall, "Our Perilous Population Implosion," *Saturday Review* September 2, 1967, p. 13.
2. Walter Kerr, *Tragedy and Comedy* (New York: Simon & Schuster, 1967), p. 138.
3. Eugene E. Jennings, "The Mobicentric Generation," *Careers Today,* January, 1969, pp. 78–79.
4. Act V, Scene 2.
5. Margaret Mead, "Cybernetics of Cybernetics," in *Purposive Systems,* ed. by H. Von Foerster, *et al.* (New York: Spartan Books, Inc., 1969), p. 4.
6. William Dixon Gray, pastor of the Downtown Presbyterian Church at Nashville, Tenn., in *The Gray Sheet,* August 11, 1968.

CHAPTER XI *Continuity and Change*

1. *The Autobiography of William Allen White* (New York: The Macmillan Co., 1946), p. 495.
2. Max L. Stackhouse, "A Theology for the New Social Gospel," in *New Theology No. 4* (New York: The Macmillan Co., 1967), p. 229.
3. John Henry C. Newman, *The Development of Christian Doctrine* (New York: Longmans, Green & Co., 1949), pp. 37–38.
4. Henry F. Lyte, "Abide with Me," *Pilgrim Hymnal* (Boston: Pilgrim Press, 1958), No. 209.

CHAPTER XII *The Case for Reparations*

1. "Repentance," *Standard Jewish Encyclopedia* (Jerusalem: Massadah Publishing Co., 1959).
2. "Restitution," *New Catholic Encyclopedia,* (New York: McGraw Hill Book Co., 1967), Vol. 12.
3. Augustus H. Strong, *Systematic Theology* (Philadelphia: Judson Press, 1907), pp. 834–35.

4. Hugh Thomas Kerr, Jr., *A Compend of Luther's Theology* (Philadelphia: Westminster Press, 1943), p. 182.
5. Malcolm X, *The Autobiography of Malcolm X* (New York: Grove Press, 1964), p. 199.
6. John Steinbeck, *The Short Reign of Pippin IV* (New York: Viking Press, 1957), pp. 146–47.

CHAPTER XIII *The Vital Balance*

1. D. R. Davies, *In Search of Myself* (New York: The Macmillan Co., 1961).
2. *Ibid*, pp. 97–98.
3. Kenneth Boulding, *The Meaning of the Twentieth Century* (New York: Harper & Row, 1964), p. 67.